THE CRESTLINE SERIES

DELIVERY TRUCKS

Donald F. Wood

MBI Publishing Company

Dedication

To Gene Olson

First published in 1999 by MBI Publishing Company, 729 Prospect Avenue, PO Box 1, Osceola, WI 54020-0001 USA

MBI Publishing Company books are also available at discounts in bulk quantity for industrial or sales-promotional use. For details write to Special Sales Manager at Motorbooks International Wholesalers & Distributors, 729 Prospect Avenue, Osceola, WI 54020-0001 USA.

Library of Congress Cataloging-in-Publication Data
Wood, Donald F.
    Delivery trucks/Donald F. Wood.
        p. cm.—(Crestline series)
    Includes bibliographical references and index.
    ISBN 0-7603-0626-5 (pbk.: alk. paper)
    1. Trucks—United States—History Pictorial works. 2. Delivery of goods—United States—History Pictorial works. I. Title. II. Series.
TL230.W656   1999
629.223'0973—dc21   99-34755

On the front cover: Top left: White House French Laundry service of San Francisco, California utilized these nifty 1961 White PDQs. *White;* Top right: Grumman Aircraft Engineering Corporation designed truck bodies under the name Aerobilt. This one is for Southern Bakeries Company. *Grumman;* Bottom left: Here's a Borden's driver/salesman making home deliveries and sales using a 1931 White with a stepvan body. *Volvo/White;* Bottom right: Hough Home Equipment Company of St. Augustine, Florida increased sales of home appliances with this Dodge Route-Van truck. Inside the truck was a display that included a gas water heater, gas clothes dryer, washing machine, electric ironer, a sink with running hot and cold water, and six wall cabinets. *Dodge*

On the back cover: Top: Three 1961 White PDQs used by a Baltimore diaper service. *Volvo/White* Center: Here we see the transition from horse to motor. A one-time horse-drawn baker's wagon had its front axle replaced by a fifth wheel so it could be pulled by this circa-1915 Ford Model T coupe. Note horn this side of steering wheel. *Fruehauf;* Bottom: A 1973 Ford C-series with an ice cream body, used by a St. Louis firm. *Aluminum Truck Bodies, St. Louis*

Designed by Bruce Leckie

Printed in the United States of America

Contents

Acknowledgments

I would like to thank the many individuals, organizations, and firms that assisted me, including: American Truck Historical Society; Phillip Baumgarten; Ruth Emerson, American Institute of Baking; Tom Garcia, Marathon Industries; The William F. Harrah Automobile Foundation; Hershey Foods Corporation; The Hoover Co.; Kathy Lau; Marshall Field & Company archives; Darwyn Nelson, Brown Cargo Van; Gabriel Phung; Jennifer Roybal, DHL; Tina Schmucker, Utilimaster; Tom Snow, Timpte; Cindy Tran; Winnie Wong; David Young; and Pauline Yu.

In addition, I would like to thank several people who generously contributed to a fund at San Francisco State University that supports old truck research. We acknowledge some of the donors: Phillip Baumgarten, Edward C. Couderc of Sausalito Moving & Storage, Gene Bills, Gilbert Hall, David Kiely, ROADSHOW, Gene Olson, Oshkosh Truck Foundation, Alvin Shaw, Art Van Aken, Charlie Wacker, Bill West, and Fred Woods. Several chapters of the American Truck Historical Society have also provided financial support to the program at San Francisco State University. The chapters include: Black Swamp, Central Coast of California, Hiawathaland, Inland Empire, Mason-Dixon, Metro Jersey, Minnesota Metro, Music City, Northeast Ohio, Shenandoah Valley, and Southern Michigan.

Donald F. Wood—San Francisco State University

Introduction

"Delivery trucks" is not a very descriptive term. Nearly any truck carrying anything must deliver it eventually. We've chosen to limit our book to cover small- and medium-size trucks that make deliveries to households and retail outlets. Delivery practices have changed over the century because of the increased, and almost universal, use of the automobile. Consumers today usually use their private autos to carry goods that their grandparents would have had delivered.

The writer was born in 1935 and recalls that milk was delivered in his neighborhood by horse-drawn wagon. An "Omar" bread man would come in a red truck, and homemakers, or their children, would rush out to where the truck was stopped and make their purchase. For a short time after World War II, the writer's parents had an ice box and, in the summer months, ice was delivered. A large card with diagonal lines from corner to corner showed how much ice the family wanted to buy. Each of the four triangles was a different color and contained the number "25," "50," "75," or "100." The card would be placed in the front window with the triangle and number on top showing the quantity needed. During winter months, we didn't buy ice; we kept food cool in a cabinet in an enclosed porch. Coal was delivered in a large truck that backed into our driveway, with the driver placing a chute down into our basement coal bin and releasing his load. Some neighbors had more difficult deliveries, two or three workers would carry metal baskets of coal on their shoulders, and dump it into the house's coal bin. Parcel post was delivered in a Ford AA mail truck. In posher neighborhoods, trucks from department stores would deliver purchases and one could also see trucks from laundries and dry cleaners.

The author also has limited experience working on delivery trucks. When only 14 or 15 years old, he rode as a helper on a truck delivering *Milwaukee Journals* to carriers and to newsstands. The job consisted of counting out the number of papers needed for the next stop, bundling them up, and either placing them on the curb or handing them to the newsstand operator.

Early in the century there were very few "chain" stores. Independent retailers were supplied by many distributors, each with their own wagon or truck. Firms with "name brands" insisted on handling all distribution aspects of their product line, a practice that continues today in beer distribution where the system is reinforced by state laws enacted after Prohibition ended.

Driver/salespersons made many of the deliveries. They were paid on a salary plus commission basis and had an incentive to sell the product they were handling. Inside a store they would also make certain that their product was attractively displayed, and they would remove any old or damaged items. They often would make a short sales pitch and leave some promotional materials, such as posters or stands for end-of-aisle displays. They would also collect payments for any products they delivered. A subtle point was whether the goods in the retail store were there "on consignment," meaning that the supplier owned them and the driver/salesperson was only collecting payment for those items the retailer had sold since the driver/salesperson's last visit. Placing goods on consignment was a common practice. Say, for example, a new tavern was opening and a snack distributor wanted to display snack products on the rack behind the bar that held bags of potato chips, salted nuts, etc. The distributor would gladly offer to supply a rack, fully stocked with products, for the bar's opening and would agree to have the driver/salesperson stop by weekly to replenish the snacks that had been sold and also collect payment for them.

The alternative to having goods on consignment is that the retailer pays for them when they are first delivered, and for replenishments. In this situation, the retailer owns the inventory.

There is also a distinction between retail deliveries and wholesale deliveries. Retail deliveries are to homes or other final users; wholesale deliveries are to retail businesses that intend to resell the items. Lars Sandberg wrote: "One of the early colonial trade institutions was the peddler who went from house to house selling such products as tin, hardware, dry goods, food, and essences used in homemade liquor. As retail stores developed, many of these peddlers assumed wholesale functions and served the retail stores, thereby becoming truck wholesalers."

At the turn of the century, most consumers reached retail stores by walking or by taking streetcars. Most retail stores had delivery services. The retail store downtown would stock items on display, the individual would make the purchase, and the goods would be delivered to his or her home directly from a warehouse. Over the century, as auto ownership grew, more and more consumers had the ability to carry goods home themselves. Suburban shopping centers, usually associated with the post–World War II era, were oriented almost completely to customers who had autos and expected to carry home nearly all purchases in their autos. Many illustrations in new car literature showed the roominess of the car's body and its ability to hold large loads of grocery bags and oversized articles.

Stores that did perform their own deliveries used their own trucks. But at the same time, delivery services developed that delivered goods for several retailers. In addition, some retailers formed cooperatives that would operate one or more trucks to deliver for all their members. Mentioned in this text but probably not emphasized sufficiently is the growth of United Parcel Service (UPS), which performs the delivery function for many businesses. Their ubiquitous brown vans, and others like them, have taken the place of delivery trucks operated by individual firms.

There were also local cartage or drayage services that would move and deliver heavier items. Many drayage companies made deliveries to and from railroad less-than-carload freight facilities. (At one time railroads offered several tiers of freight service. Railway Express was run cooperatively by all railroads and was carried on express package cars hauled on passenger trains. Less-than-carload freight service consisted of mixed freight carried on railcars in freight trains, and was handled through sheds at each city's freight terminal. Carload service—still offered—consists of carloads carried directly from shippers' sidings to consignees' sidings.)

One truck type associated with deliveries is the stand-up van, or step-van, or walk-in van. The driving compartment is higher so that the driver can stand while driving and often the controls are arranged so that the truck can be driven with the driver either sitting or standing. When making frequent deliveries, the driver would stand while driving; for longer hops he or she would sit. Some trucks could be driven while the operator was standing on the right side even though the steering wheel was on the left.

The term "forward control" is applied to chassis used in step-van applications, although most of them can be driven in the conventional manner only. The term is somewhat relative, in that it means that the driver's seat is closer to the front than it would be in that maker's conventional truck chassis.

Many truck chassis builders produced chassis that could be outfitted with stand-up vans by a number of outfitters. Often the chassis make is not easily identifiable in photos, and readers will note that some photo captions given here are remarkably imprecise.

The early makers of autos and trucks often produced a "commercial chassis" which included the chassis, powertrain, and bodywork back to the cowl. These chassis were then delivered to a body builder who would complete the body, paint it, and deliver it to the user. Auto and truck builders also built some popular bodies themselves, such as for pickup and panel trucks. Or, they might contract with a body builder to complete, say, 2,000 3/4-ton trucks with utility bodies, and then the truck dealer would sell the completed trucks.

Truck body builders are used for many specialized body needs, and a much wider range of individual truck body styles exists than most would imagine. Here is a list of delivery and service bodies from the mid-1950s, taken from a Chevrolet truck *The Silver Book* (a catalog of parts, bodies, and other equipment made by others to fit Chevrolet chassis, and marketed through Chevrolet truck dealers). They are: "A" frame glass-carrying, acid tanks, air compressors, armored car, asphalt tank, bakery, beer, beverage, bookmobiles, bottlers, brick-loading/unloading, bulk cement, cable splicers, canopy, cargo van, cattle rack, cement mixer, chest X-ray, cleaners and dyers, clinic (mobile), coal, concrete, contractors, dairy, delivery, dental clinic, department store, dry freight, dump, electric meter installer's, express, florists, food products, frozen foods, fuel oil, furniture, gas cylinder, gas meter installation, gasoline transport, grocers', high-lift, ice, ice cream, insulated, laundry, lumber, machine shop, meat packers, milk delivery, painters', pallet-loading, parcel delivery, pie distributors', plumbers', produce, public utility service, radio units, refrigerator, self-unloading, street light maintenance, telephone installation, tree trimmer, and wrecker. A list of specialized trailers and semi-trailers was about half as long and listed many of the same applications.

There are other body types associated with deliveries and they reflect the characteristics of the materials being handled. Also included are a few pictures of trucks used by workers in residential areas.

A device developed for operating a Ford TT ice delivery truck from the rear. Driver stands on rear platform and can steer. The tiller-handle device closest to us must control the trucks starting and stopping. *American Automobile Manufacturers Association*

Chapter One

1901–1910

The home delivery system was well in place before the advent of the auto. Jack D. Rittenhouse's book *American Horse-Drawn Vehicles* contains illustrations of several types of horse-drawn delivery wagons. They include a milk wagon, merchant's wagon, baker's wagon, butcher wagon "with steak boxes, cutting block, meat hooks," ice wagon, beer wagon, coal wagon, oil tank wagon, pie wagon, wholesale grocery wagon, berry or fruit rack wagon, market wagon, furniture wagon, and dry-goods wagon. The wagon styles just listed were used primarily for deliveries; heavy wagons were used to move larger shipments of freight. Many of the heavier wagons were referred to as "drays," and today the term "drayage" refers to hauling freight within urban areas.

According to Professor Edward P. Duggan of Goucher College, the beginning of the century there were 7,632 carriage and wagon factories and custom and repair shops, that made at least five vehicles a year, in the United States. Of these, 99 employed between 101 and 250 workers each, and 32 had between 251 and 1,000 employees.

Many of the wagon builders who built the styles of wagons described above soon adapted to building similar bodies and fitting them on auto or truck chassis. Hackney Bros. of Wilson, North Carolina, had been building wagons since before the Civil War. They made their entry into truck bodies when they adapted one of their standard horse-drawn milk bodies to fit on a local dairy's Ford Model T from which another body had been removed.

The Wren and Wren book *Motor Trucks of America* is a valuable compendium of the motor truck and its adaptation to many uses. Here are some of the early highlights they note:

1897 A Chicago firm built and sold two electric delivery vehicles to a silk merchant.

Munson autos and light trucks were built in LaPorte, Indiana, between 1896 and 1900. Here's their delivery wagon. Power was provided by a gas/electric engine. *American Truck Historical Society*

1898 Several firms buy electric delivery wagons; Consolidated Ice Co. of New York, asks for bids to convert 1,000 horse-driven wagons to power-driven vehicles.

1899 The U.S. post office begins experimenting with powered vehicles.

1900 White Brothers introduced a steam-powered delivery truck. New York City newspapers begin using electric trucks for newspaper distribution.

1903 In New York City, test trials were held to determine truck dependability. Entered were six steam, four gasoline, and one electric. The Knox, with an air-cooled gasoline engine, performed the best.

1904 A total of 700 trucks were built, most were electric.

1905 Anheuser-Busch's fleet totalled 35 trucks.

1909 The H. C. Piercy Company, which handled deliveries for 80 New York merchants, ordered 25 Studebaker electric delivery trucks to replace 300 horses and 200 wagons.

1910 Truck production totaled 6,000 units.

At the end of the first decade of the twentieth century, trucks had made inroads into delivery markets. At first, electric trucks seemed better adapted than gasoline-powered trucks to replace the horse in urban markets. An article in the March 4, 1904, issue of the *Dry Goods Reporter* quoted the manager of Marshall Field's shipping department: "We use only electric machines as the odor of gasoline, in our opinion, injures the goods."

By 1910, however, Gimbel Brothers in New York had a fleet of 88 gasoline trucks. The auto was still little more than a curiosity to most, although in 1909 Henry Ford had introduced his Model T and popularity of the auto would explode in the following decade.

The trade magazine *The Commercial Carrier Journal* published its 75th anniversary issue in March 1986 and listed milestones of trucking by decade. Some they listed for this early decade include: recognition of superiority of steering wheel over tiller, the sealed universal joint, Weed tire chains, Prestolite gas headlights, belt-driven engine cooling pumps, and demountable rims.

An article in the April 17, 1937, issue of *Baker's Helper* looked back at the industry's early days and reported: "Ward-Corby Co., Chicago, were utilizing electric trucks made by the Pittsburgh Motor Vehicle Co. in 1910. In Birmingham, Alabama, it was reported that Fisch & Malchow, Highland Bakery, were operating the first commercial auto in the sunny South used by a bakery."

UPS began as a messenger service in Seattle in 1907 and continued to grow throughout the century, taking over the delivery and trucking functions of much of the U.S. economy.

In 1900 the Hershey firm purchased this Riker Electric, built in Elizabethtown, New Jersey. According to the company, the vehicle was purchased to attract attention and make people think that the chocolate company was modern and up-to-date. After the people in Lancaster, Pennsylvania, became accustomed to its presence, it was sent to other Pennsylvania cities served by salespeople with order-books in hand. *Hershey Foods*

A three-wheeled Knox delivery rig, from about 1902. The Knox was built in Springfield, Massachusetts. *Baker Library, Harvard University*

A Locodelivery, built by Locomobile in about 1902. It was steam powered and its water tank held 50 gallons. Locomobiles were built in Watertown, Massachusetts. *Baker Library, Harvard University*

Delivering the mail would be a major task requiring many trucks. Here's one of the post office's very first trucks, a circa-1905 Johnson steamer, built in Milwaukee. *Johnson Controls*

A circa-1908 Grabowsky used by a dry cleaner. Note the crank, chain drive, right-hand steering, and roof rack. Grabowksy trucks were built in Detroit and the firm would become part of General Motors. *American Automobile Manufacturers Association*

A telephone installer unloads a new telephone from the rear of a 1908 Holsman, built in Chicago. This rig is steered by a tiller. *Western Electric Photographic Services*

This is a 1908 Sternberg, used by a Seattle candy company. Sternberg trucks, built in Milwaukee, later became Sterlings. *The William F. Harrah Automobile Foundation*

A 1908 Studebaker electric delivery truck. Its range was 35 miles and it could go at speeds from 2 to 9 miles per hour. Studebaker was headquartered in South Bend, Indiana. *Antique Studebaker Club*

This coal peddler has filled his wagon with coal from a railcar, which he will now peddle from door to door. *Missouri Valley Room, Kansas City Public Library*

Automobiles were also used for making deliveries. We see a 1909–10 Hudson coupe, delivering bundled newspapers. *American Automobile Manufacturers Association*

In the early days, many trucks were sold as chassis and the buyer then had to make separate arrangements to have a body built. Here, at a 1910 truck show, we see a Geneva chassis in the foreground and behind is a similar chassis upon which an enclosed panel body has been built. The Geneva Wagon Co. was located in Geneva, New York, and survived until about 1920. *American Automobile Manufacturers Association*

A circa-1909 Reo flareboard with a load of hay on an urban street. In this era cities were good markets for hay because so many horses were still stabled there. Reos were built in Lansing. *American Truck Historical Society*

Chapter Two

1911–1920

Many of the photos in this book show Fords. They were extremely popular and, in some years, accounted for nearly half of all truck registrations. Viewing old newsreels or movies with street scenes, one sees Fords pictured almost exclusively. Their popularity cannot be overestimated. (Indeed, just after World War I, the Ford Model Ts assembled in Manchester, England, outnumbered all other makes on the roads of Britain.)

An ad in the 1912 *Commercial Car Journal* (now the *Commercial Carrier Journal*) was for a Ford Model T delivery car, which sold for $700, with the price including brass windshield, speedometer, Ford Magneto built into the motor, two 6-inch gas lamps and gas generator, three oil lamps, and tools. Part of the text of the ad said:

> We did not offer the Ford Model T Delivery Car to the business world until we had thoroughly tried it out in the very line of work that business makes for

a Delivery Car. Now—after two years of experience in delivering merchandise—two years over city streets of all sorts—over country roads—in hilly territory—in all sorts of weather—winter and summer—we know this car 'will deliver the goods.' We therefore recommend the Ford Model T Delivery Car with our broadest warranty as a dependable, economical, durable, convenient, money-saving delivery car—for the big store, for the little store— for the city, town, village or country.

An article in a 1911 issue of *Scientific American* compared the relative efficiencies of motor trucks and horses. They cited one month's records of a dry goods company in Allentown, Pennsylvania, that operated several horse-drawn wagons and an International "high wheeler" delivery truck. For the motor truck the costs were driver's wages, $60.00; boy's wages, $24.00; gasoline at 14 cents a gallon, $27.69, oil, $7.31; and repairs, $9.45; totalling $128.45. The motor truck could do the work of two horse-drawn wagons. Costs for the two wagons were drivers' wages, $104.00; boys wages, $32.00; and feed for horses, $35.00; totalling $171.00. The article's author commented upon this report by adding: "The foregoing showing is the more remarkable because while repairs to the motor wagons are included, no item appears for repairs to the horse wagons or harness or for shoeing. The same firm states that the average cost per month for the motor wagon for fuel, oil, rent and repairs is $20.00, as against $50.00 for food, rent, shoeing, and repairs for a two-horse service."

In 1913, Kroger replaced their horse and wagon teams with 75 Ford Model T trucks. Many of these were used for home deliveries. (As a "chain" store, Kroger also needed trucks to supply its own stores. Later, it developed its own bakeries and meat processing

Tawrie Wagon & Carriage Co. of Winnipeg built this body for a dyeing and dry cleaning company. *Manitoba Archives*

plants, and had fleets making direct deliveries to stores from these plants, as well as from its warehouses.)

Milk deliveries were probably the most common of all deliveries in this era. Houses and apartment houses usually had a milk compartment that had two doors, one opening outside for the milkman; the other opening inside. The customer would leave clean empty bottles in the box along with a card that was marked with the order for the day of milk, cream, butter, etc. The milkman would collect the empties, leave the order, and mark in the route book the items delivered that day. Once a month or so the milkman would collect payment.

The milkman who made these home deliveries was a driver/salesperson. Another important person in this distribution network was the driver/salesperson's immediate superior, the route foreman. The route foreman had many duties: supervising, hiring, training, firing, finding new customers, regaining lost customers, substituting for absent driver/salespersons, helping resolve disputes with customers, and handling details of sales promotion campaigns.

Wren and Wren reported the following for this period:

1911   The first national truck show was held at Madison Square Garden. Displayed were 27 gasoline trucks; 7 electric trucks; and 18 motorcycles.
1912   Truck body designs began extending the roof over the driver, yielding some protection from elements.
1913   A survey showed that brewers were the biggest users of trucks.
1914   Macy and Company retained researchers from the Massachusetts Institute of Tech-

nology to determine the best method to serve Macy's 2,500-square-mile delivery territory.
1915   Production totalled 74,000 trucks.
1916   At least 19 different body builders produced stock model bodies that fit Ford Model T chassis.
1918   The Council of National Defense asked retail stores to limit their deliveries to one a day to help conserve resources for the war effort.
1919   Enclosed cabs with sliding doors appeared on many trucks. The International Retail Delivery Association endorsed the principle of one delivery per day.
1920   Refrigerated bodies utilizing brine were introduced. Truck production climbed to 322,000 units.

Wren and Wren noted a truck show in New York City in 1911. It was followed by a show in Chicago that lasted several days. The February 7 issue of the *Chicago Tribune* said: "Many of the exhibitors follow a plan of showing [commercial] cars on which are lettered the names of well-known business firms who have ordered vehicles, and the plan seems to be proving

The rear view shows compartments in the body. *Navistar Archives*

A chocolate candy maker used this circa-1911 International "high wheeler." *Navistar Archives*

a good one. There are so many of the cars with business firm names painted upon them that show visitors interested in almost any line of business can find in the Coliseum a number of delivery wagons and trucks that are to be used by various firms in the same lines."

The *Commercial Carrier Journal's* 75th anniversary issue listed these developments during the decade: pneumatic tires, semi-trailers, steel wheels, tire retreaders, self-starters, air brakes, electric lights, windshield wipers, and closed cabs. They also reported that in 1912 there were 461 different makes of trucks.

Earlier we had mentioned that the truck chassis had to be shipped to the body builder for comple-

tion. An article in a 1919 issue of the *Commercial Car Journal* noted that some truck dealers were beginning to stock standardized bodies as a sideline, installing them themselves and profiting on both their sale and installation. Bodies were becoming more standardized, as were trucks. (Part of the standardization of trucks came as a result of World War I, when the lack of standardization had made it difficult for the military to maintain trucks.) At various times, body builders would also keep some popular models of truck chassis in stock so that buyers would not have to wait for a chassis to be delivered to the body builder.

This CT Electric, dating from before World War I, was delivering ice in Puerto Rico into the 1950s. CTs were built by the Commercial Truck Company of Philadelphia. *Smithsonian Institution*

For the first half of the century, major urban areas in the United States were served by rail transit lines that connected many major cities as well as cities and their suburbs. They were known as "interurbans." These interurban lines were in addition to passenger trains and local streetcars. Some interurban lines carried freight, such as the one shown here with a 1910–11 White backed up to the railcar door. *Volvo/White*

A Hesse body on an early-teens Ford Model T used to deliver groceries. Note the lines of the rear fenders. *Hesse Corporation*

Wagenhals delivery vehicles were built in St. Louis between 1910 and 1914. The vehicles had two wheels in front and one in the rear. The nameplate refers to it as "special delivery." Note that the driver sat in the rear. Initial models were electric; the firm then switched to gasoline engines. *American Automobile Manufacturers Association*

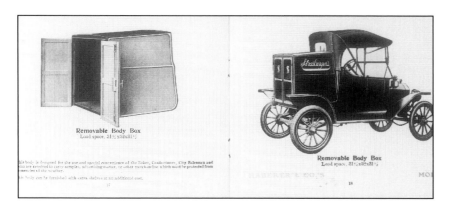

Removable Body Box
Load space, 31½x32x31½

Removable Body Box
Load space, 31½x32x31½

An enclosed body built to fit on the rear of Ford Model Ts, circa 1913. The builder was Haberer & Co. and the body was "designed for the use and special convenience of the baker, confectioner...." *The William F. Harrah Automobile Foundation*

An article in a 1913 trade journal suggested the use of containers that would be carried on large flatbed trailers to distribution points where they would be loaded aboard individual, smaller trucks. The distribution point is a shed, so not all trucks need be present simultaneously. *The William F. Harrah Automobile Foundation*

The LAUTH-JUERGENS MOTOR CAR CO.

Royal Garden TEAS   THE BOUR CO.   High Grade COFFEES.

Model "G" One-Ton Truck, with Special Wire Body

A circa-1913 Lauth-Juergens with a roof and screen mesh sides, used by a coffee and tea distributor. The truck builder was located in Fremont, Ohio. *Hendrickson Mfg. Co.*

Three circa-1914 Pierce-Arrows ready to deliver ice. Each truck has a driver and two helpers. Pierce-Arrows were built in Buffalo. *Smithsonian Institution*

A 1914 Lauth-Juergens with a furniture body. *Hendrickson Mfg. Co.*

This 1914 Service delivered parcel post packages in Indianapolis. Service trucks were made in Wabash, Indiana. *Ron Woodward*

A circa-1914 White truck being used to resupply a horse-drawn ice wagon. As trucks were being introduced into delivery systems, they were first used in resupply operations such as this. *Volvo/White*

Armleder trucks were built in Cincinnati, which is also the headquarters for Kroger. At one time Kroger had a fleet of trucks for home deliveries but this size of truck was more likely used to make deliveries from a warehouse to a retail store. The truck is from about 1915. *The Kroger Co.*

Here's an early form of containerization, used by a wholesale grocer. The container is on the left and is being pulled onto the truck's frame. There appear to be rollers built into the body and a power take-off drum at the rear of the truck's frame. Having multiple containers freed trucks so they could be hauling rather than waiting to be loaded, item by item. *Press Tank & Equipment Co., Chicago*

A circa-1915 Dorris, used for distributing a St. Louis newspaper. Dorris trucks were built in St. Louis between 1906 and 1927. *McCabe-Powers Body Co.*

Here we see the transition from horse to motor. A onetime horse-drawn baker's wagon had its front axle replaced by a fifth wheel so it could be pulled by this circa-1915 Ford Model T coupe. Note the horn on this side of the steering wheel. *Fruehauf*

In areas with snow, a sled replaced the wagon during winter months. This rig was operated by Freihofer Bakery. *Freihofer*

A Jeffery with a panel body, circa 1915. The firm, located in Kenosha, Wisconsin, would soon become better known because of its Quads, built for World War I. The firm became part of Nash. *American Automobile Manufacturers Association*

Kissel trucks were built in Hartford, Wisconsin. This 3/4-ton model was used to deliver ice in Providence, Rhode Island. It has right-hand steering and a single acetylene lamp mounted on the dash, and lanterns on either side of the cowl. *Smithsonian Institution*

A circa-1916 White carrying bagged coal.
Volvo/White

In 1917 Ford came out with its truck model, the TT. In addition, a number of "extendo" kits were sold which allowed the user to extend and reinforce the truck's frame. Note this Ford has a longer wheelbase than those pictured to this point. The cab is called a "C cab" because of its shape. *The William F. Harrah Automobile Foundation*

This circa-1917 International was used by a baker. *Navistar Archives*

The rear view shows where trays or shelves would be placed. *Navistar Archives*

The truck is a Hewitt Ludlow (built in San Francisco) and it's carrying bulk vinegar. There is a spigot at the rear of the tank. Our guess is this was a wholesaler who would sell in bulk to retail grocers. *L. Jonson*

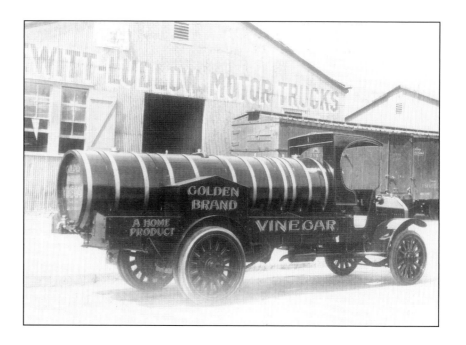

THE VIM TRUCK

Vim trucks were made in Philadelphia. This 1917 model was used by Gimbel's department store for deliveries. *Chuck Rhoads*

This is one of the earliest Chevrolets, circa 1918; it was used by a laundry. *Oregon Historical Society*

A World War I–era White delivering a load of bricks, probably for paving. *Volvo/White*

A 1919 Packard truck being loaded with large blocks of ice. *Smithsonian Institution*

Two circa-1919 Whites used by Heinz for deliveries to grocery wholesalers. Note the additional fender amidship under each truck. *H. J. Heinz*

A circa-1920 Hendrickson panel truck with solid tires used by a sausage maker. Hendrickson trucks were built in Chicago until recently. *Hendrickson Mfg. Co.*

A screenside panel body, built by Giant, on a Samson chassis, circa 1920. Samson trucks were built in Janesville, Wisconsin. *Giant Manufacturing Co.*

Autos with trailers also made some freight deliveries although relatively few pictures exist of auto-drawn trailers used for freight deliveries. This picture shows an auto-drawn trailer used for delivering lumber. The front of the bed unlocks from the tongue, the load tips backward, and the auto and trailer drive slowly forward until clear of the load. *Utility Trailer Manufacturing Co.*

Stewart trucks were made in Buffalo. This one was delivering a large gas oven.

Chapter Three

1921–1930

In a Hackney Bros. company history, two old-timers were asked about plant activity in the 1920s. They said that the company's major products were cabs and flats. The cabs were built on truck chassis and came in three styles. One was open with optional storm curtains; one was enclosed with hinged doors; and the best model had the hinged doors with roll-up windows. "Flats" were platform bodies, with varying arrangements of stakes, gates, and roof bows. The firm also built "express" bodies (similar to pickup bodies today) for mounting behind the cab. Express bodies came with and without canopy tops.

Trucks usually went through at least two painting processes. The first would be the painting of the chassis and cab at the chassis manufacturer's, and then the painting of the completed rig, after the body had been fitted. At this point, pictures, stripes, and lettering would be applied. (Gold leaf might be used and the gold leaf would be varnished over to protect it.) An article in a 1925 issue of the *Automobile Trimmer and Painter,* "The Possibilities In Colors For Truck Advertising," discussed a number of points. One concern was whether the user was in a trade where trucks were washed regularly; if not, darker colors were recommended. An example was given of coal trucks painted black with gold lettering, with the choice of gold conveying the suggestion of glowing coals. Laundries, bake shops, confectioners, and grocers were advised to use white or other light colors. Trucks used by tea and coffee companies were to be the same colors as used on their retail packages, and produce vendors' trucks were to be painted shades of garden green. For stores with products aimed at a higher class customer, the article recommended truck "colors suggestive of the mellow, soulful, restful, qualities . . . blue, purple, violet—those command attention."

The last step in painting the truck was the addition of hand lettering and striping. Imagination was a useful tool to the truck painter. An article in a 1930 issue of the *Automobile Trimmer and Painter* entitled "How to Develop Profitable Commercial Fleet Business" gave these examples of how some jobs had been obtained by enterprising auto painters:

> In San Francisco a certain printing house makes a specialty of color work. The concern was approached by an automobile painter who suggested that its delivery truck could be used as a fitting advertisement for this specialty. He devised a color scheme, splashes of color in modernistic manner and landed the order.
>
> Another San Francisco establishment specializes in the manufacture of window blinds. An automobile painter was approached with the request that he work out some idea whereby the delivery trucks operated by that concern should

Stoughton Wagon Co. offered this furniture body for Fords. It has screen sides and storm curtains. *The William F. Harrah Automobile Foundation*

advertise the service in a highly attractive manner. The painter designed a color scheme in black and white. One half of the body was painted black, the other half white. In a conspicuous place on each side of the body the following was lettered in: "A blind man drives this truck."

Many truck owners had more than one truck and wished to have them painted in a uniform manner. This uniformity was achieved in a number of ways. One was by fleet painting charts, which were "to-scale" drawings showing exactly what was to be painted where, and in what colors. Within the body shop, patterns were drawn on heavy paper, which was then laid flat on a soft, even surface. A small pinwheel device was then rolled along the lines, leaving a pattern of perforations.

This White armored truck, from the early 1920s, delivered payrolls. The workers would walk up to the platform in the rear of the truck and receive their pay envelopes. *Mack Museum*

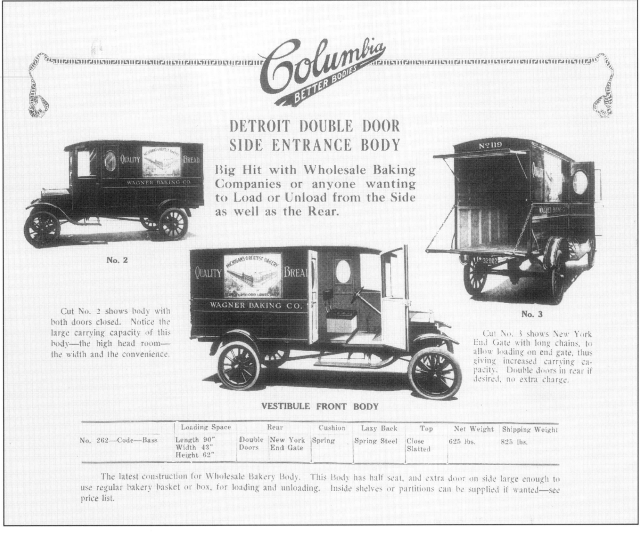

This is an ad for the Columbia wholesale bakery body for Ford Model TT chassis. Double doors on the curb side are to facilitate unloading. *Ford Archives*

This pattern was then taped on the side of the truck and dusted with chalk. A pattern of dots marked the lines to be followed by the painter. This pattern could be re-used.

Another way to achieve uniformity was to prepare baked enamel aluminum sign panels, and then attach them to the truck. This had several advantages. The first was that truck "down-time" was reduced because the truck would be tied up only long enough to rivet on the sign. Through silkscreen processes any number of sign panels could be prepared, and even shipped to other sites.

A variation of this, found mainly on newspaper trucks, was a metal frame that enclosed a heavy paper poster which would be changed every week or so. Mail, REA Express, and some telephone trucks carried these changeable posters.

A final development, and one still in use today, was the application of decalcomania transfers. These would be designed for each customer's needs, and printed in batches; the decal transfer printer could produce any needed quantity.

Before application there would be two layers to the sheet: the decal and its backing. The sheet would be applied to a clean surface on the truck and the backing removed, leaving the decal in place. All sorts of pictures, symbols, and letters could be printed on decal transfers, and in more detail than could be accomplished by the sign painter. The sign painter was still needed for providing local information, such as the firm's phone number.

Some highlights of this decade, recorded by Wren and Wren, included:

1922 Rolling grocery stores were being introduced into many communities but encountering quick opposition from established retail merchants who paid real estate taxes. American Railway Express was operating 800 vehicles in the New York City area.

1923 GMC offered an open express body with or without top and with an open or closed cab. Previously, GMC had sold only chassis.

1925 The Pak-Age-Car was introduced at the Chicago Delivery Truck Show, and it had an engine and transmission at the end of the chassis. Truck production was 531,000 trucks.

1926 The Electric Truck Manufacturers Association disbanded.

1927 The Dodge Bros. coupes and roadster models offered telescoping drawers in the rear of the auto.

1929 Chevrolet added a sedan delivery to its offering of trucks. Production for 1929 was 882,000 trucks.

1930 Truck production dropped to 575,000 units because of the Depression.

An article in the September 1929 issue of the *Commercial Car Journal* dealt with the relative costs of horses and motor trucks for route deliveries. Some excerpts follow: "Variety of products served from one vehicle make the horse's knowledge of his route of less and less importance. In fact it places the horse at a disadvantage under certain conditions. . . . When a driver finds a note in a milk bottle ordering something additional, as a dozen eggs, he may be compelled to chase down the street to the wagon which the horse obligingly has pulled up to the next stop. The cost of getting a horse to and from a route is of major importance. There is a direct loss of time of about 12 minutes for each 5280 feet of dead mileage. Such losses take place on all routes except those originating in branches, and increase as distance from branch becomes greater. This lost time handicaps sales extension plans. Indirect cost of maintaining branches close enough together to keep this dead mileage at a reasonable figure runs into a lot of money."

In the *Commercial Carrier Journal's* 75th anniversary issue are mentioned these developments during the decade: mechanical cooling devices that relied on the slow release of compressed cooled gas, four-wheel air brakes, ethylene glycol–based antifreeze, voltage regulators, and other instrument gauges that allowed the operator to better monitor the engine. Six-cylinder, rather than four-cylinder engines were now more common, and chain drive was on its way out.

The silo-type structure is a bat roost and the bat droppings, known as guano, are collected at the bottom, bagged, and sold for fertilizer. The truck is a Ford Model TT. *Express-Nears Collection, Institute of Texan Culture*

An early-1920s Ford Model TT used by a laundry in Birmingham, Alabama. Holes in the tires were to give a cushioning effect. *O.V. Hunt Collection, Birmingham Public Library, Birmingham, Alabama*

A panel body built by Giant on an early-1920s Samson. *Giant Manufacturing Co.*

An interior view. Note curvature. *Giant Manufacturing Co.*

This is one of 276 Walker Electrics operated by Marshall Field & Company, the famous Chicago department store. This one has a customs house license number so it may have been used to haul imports after they cleared customs at a port. Walker Electrics were manufactured in Chicago. *Marshall Field's*

Kelland trucks were built from 1922 until 1925, in Newark, New Jersey. They were electric. This one was used by a laundry in Jersey City. *The William F. Harrah Automobile Foundation*

Sales of ice and coal complemented each other. Here we see a Heil body on an early-1920s Ford Model TT. Note the ice tongs on the left. *The Heil Co.*

This is a mid-1920s Gramm-Bernstein used by a bread company. Gramm-Bernstein trucks were built in Lima, Ohio. *University of Michigan*

National Guardsmen congregate around a Ford Model T with a slip-on body carrying Carnation milk in the early 1920s. *Carnation*

Traveling stores did not make individual deliveries, but they did make scheduled stops at specific intersections and homemakers would then make their purchases. This one, on a mid-1920s International chassis, was used by a delicatessen in Camden, New Jersey. *Navistar Archives*

Interior view of the traveling store. There's a "lip" at the bottom of each shelf and they apparently tip downward away from the truck's center. *Navistar Archives*

A 1924 Kenworth used to carry the mail. Its screened body has a double door on the curb side. *Paccar*

For a brief period, Yellow trucks were offered by the taxicab manufacturer. This 1924 model with an open C-cab was used by Upjohn for delivering drugs. *Upjohn*

A mid-1920s Chevrolet panel, with the cutout of a bottle on its side, at a loading ramp. *Hoard Museum, Fort Atkinson, Wisconsin*

A mid-1920s Gotfredson panel truck, made in Detroit, with a sign on the side saying "originators of the ice cream soda." *Fred Sanders, Inc.*

Orpha Sutherland stands in front of a circa-1925 Ford Model T used by her husband John for promoting the sale of Shredded Wheat in Western Canada. John Sutherland's sales territory included the Provinces of British Columbia, Alberta, Saskatchewan, and Manitoba. In the spring he would start out from Vancouver on a southerly route (sometimes relying on the railroad to carry his Ford on a flatcar over the Rockies) and work his way east to Winnipeg. He would distribute samples of Shredded Wheat in small boxes (two biscuits each). He'd take orders, which would be shipped to the grocers via rail. Sutherland would also pick up new supplies of samples that would be waiting for him at railheads. After reaching Winnipeg he would head west, before winter came. During winter months, he travelled on passenger railroads. John's son remembers his father telling of being in the Ford once while it was surrounded by buffalo, and waiting very quietly. John also stated that the Ford was very durable and well-built to hold up under the road and travel conditions of that era. Note tire chains on the spare tire. *Jack and Marilyn Sutherland*

Here's the choice of cab styles for Ford commercial chassis offered by Hackney Brothers of Wilson, North Carolina. *Hackney Bros. Body Co.*

A mid-1920s International used by a baker. *Charles Wacker Co.*

Washing some mid-1920s Internationals in the Bowman dairy fleet. Milk trucks were almost always painted white and kept very clean. *Navistar Archives*

A Kenworth milk truck from the mid-1920s. Cases would be stowed inside the body. *Paccar*

Motorcycles were once widely used for deliveries (and were the subject for an article by the author in a 1986 issue of *American Motorcyclist*). This one delivered new tires in Birmingham. O.V. Hunt Collection, *Birmingham Public Library, Birmingham, Alabama*

Two parked delivery trucks in a 1926 photo. The one on the left distributes barbers' supplies for the Rialto Barber Supply Co. The truck on the right is operated by Carmack's Pressing Service and has windows and an open vent on the roof. The sign on the side says "Pressing at Your Door," apparently meaning the work is done inside the truck body. *National Archives*

A seed company used this 1926 Garford with a covered body. Garford trucks were built in Garford, Ohio. *Oregon Historical Society*

Double-parked trucks are nothing new. Here we see two double-parked trucks making deliveries in the late 1920s. At center is a coal truck that has elevated its body, and on the far side men are carrying large metal buckets (about the size of bushel baskets) of coal. At far right is an electric truck. *National Archives*

A 1927 GMC, with cowl-mounted headlights, used by Hormel to distribute its meat products. *Hormel*

A Walker electric truck, delivering ice in Laredo, Texas, in the late 1920s. *Central Power & Light, Corpus Christi*

A 1928 Brockway panel truck, used by a Boston creamery. Brockways were built in Cortland, New York, until the 1970s. *Brockway*

This late-1920s photo shows trucks at a produce market. In this situation, the farmers' trucks do not make individual deliveries. Instead, they all drive to the same site, display their produce, and sell to individual consumers who come to the market. *Utah Division of State History*

A late-1920s electric truck used to distribute Omar bread. *Omar*

Prior to World War II, the United States was served by a vast network of passenger-carrying railroads. Passenger railroads owned cooperatively a firm known as "Railway Express Agency" and carried its parcels between cities on express cars that ran as part of passenger trains. The firm was better known as REA. It used trucks for local pickups and deliveries of freight. This REA truck is a Ward Electric, from the late 1920s. *American Automobile Manufacturers Association*

A Divco Model G, introduced in 1929, used by a dairy. The driver is demonstrating how to operate the truck while standing on the right side. The truck could be operated from either running board. Divcos were built in Detroit. *Carnation*

Detroit's Dyko Drive Corporation built this device for step-vans that allowed the driver to use only one pedal while standing to either move or stop the vehicle. This could be done with either foot, and a single pedal activated both the brake and the clutch. The driver could also use the truck's conventional controls while seated.

This Fageol, with custom headlights, turn-indicator arrows, and big shocks, was operated by United Parcel Service in Southern California. It has 1929 California plates. Fageols were built in Oakland until just before World War II. *UPS*

A Model A Ford sedan delivery that was recently restored by See's Candies of San Francisco. It appears in local parades.

A Ford AA with a long wheelbase, used by a laundry. The body was built by McCabe-Powers of St. Louis. *McCabe-Powers Body Co.*

The lettering on the door says "advertising car," meaning that this truck carried advertising materials that would be used to build and stock Coca-Cola promotional displays. The white-gloved ladies have "Coca-Cola" emblems on their caps. *Lorin Sorensen*

A 1929 Reo panel truck, used by Squibb's for delivering dental products to pharmacies. *Squibb & Sons*

A circa-1929 Kleiber used by an ice and cold storage company. "Cold storage" meant that the company had an ice-cooled warehouse that could be used to store meat and produce. Kleiber trucks were built in San Francisco. *Smithsonian Institution*

Note the landau lights on the sides of this 1929 Reo panel truck used to make deliveries for Stix, Baer & Fuller, a department store. *McCabe-Powers Body Co.*

A 1929 White used by an industrial laundry in Los Angeles. Four men are engaged in the unloading process. *Volvo/White*

This is an REA publicity photo showing rail/truck/air linkages. On the Rock Island train, packages are being unloaded from the express car. *REA*

This Ford AA carried Alhambra bottled water in the San Francisco area. *Fabco*

A circa-1930 Kleiber used by a northern California ice-cream maker. *National Automotive History Collection, Detroit Public Library*

Three circa-1930 Sterlings operated by the Exhibitors' Service Company of Pittsburgh. The firm was a "film carrier," later recognized as a special classification of carriers by the Interstate Commerce Commission. At the time, movie theaters would place the films they were done showing in a locked box where the film carrier would pick them up and also drop off the films to be shown next. Banners on these trucks promote films. Most of the trucking operations were at night. Service was faster than other motor carriers and these trucks also carried some perishable food and morning newspapers. Film needed special handling because theaters would advertise their next show before the film was in their hands. Also, until the 1950s, film was nitrate-based and, as it deteriorated, became explosive. *Exhibitors' Service Company*

Bullock's Wilshire store in Southern California used these two 1930 Studebakers. The driver's compartment is open, and there are landau lights, similar to limousines of that era. *American Automobile Manufacturers Association*

Thorne trucks were stand-up vans built in Chicago between 1929 and 1938. They were powered by a Buda engine which supplied electricity to the motor that propelled the wheels. This is a 1930 model, in need of restoration. It had originally been owned by Reids Union Dairy in Brooklyn, New York. *American Truck Historical Society*

We see a Borden's White tractor with a flatbed trailer, built by Highway, carrying three electric milk trucks. The fact that the tractor trailer has Borden's markings suggests that the rig was used daily to carry the short-range electric trucks between the bottling plant and their routes. *Volvo/White*

A 1930 White Model 60K intended for use as a milk wagon. *Volvo/White*

Chapter Four

1931–1940

The 1930s was probably the single most important decade in the history of trucks. By the decade's end, trucks were nearly as developed as they are today and were in widespread use. They were also streamlined, more so than would be the case after World War II. This chapter contains many more illustrations than the others, because this was probably the most important decade for delivery trucks. In the next decade, World War II would take place, and in the peacetime that followed, Americans would spread out into the suburbs with shopping centers and become much less dependent upon delivery truck service.

In the late 1920s, a deluxe style of delivery body came into use, which I have referred to elsewhere as "boulevard delivery." Their front ends, up through the driver's open compartment, looked like that of a limousine. Many had landau lights mounted high, just behind the driver's compartment. In 1932 an auto and truck body builders' trade magazine said: "In increasing numbers on the streets of our larger cities are appearing some very stylish delivery cars with bodies patterned after the very latest fine coach designs. There is always a certain class of particular buyers who are interested in such special jobs and willing to pay the extra costs."

Many firms operated large fleets of trucks. Here's a 1931 list of large fleets, prepared by the National Automobile Chamber of Commerce: A, T & T, 15,500; Standard Oil (New Jersey), 12,000; Borden Co., 10,000; Railway Express Agency, 9,247; Post Office Department, 8,450; Standard Oil (Indiana), 7,465; Mid-West Utilities, 3,881; Continental Baking Co., 3,500; Standard Brands, 3,275; Standard Oil (California), 2,677; Gulf Refining, 2,262; Ward Baking Co., 2,240; Commonwealth & Southern, 2,103; Standard Oil (New York), 2,098; Armour and Co., 1,973; General Baking Co., 1,856; Shell Petroleum Corporation,

This was on the cover of a piece of literature showing the Chevrolet-Montpelier "side-aisle" delivery trucks, circa 1931. *Smithsonian Institution*

1,542; and American Ice Co., 1,487. Farther down on the list were Western Dairy Products, 1,015; Sheffield Farms, 900; American Stores Co., 682; United Parcel Service, 510; R. H. Macy & Co., 415; Pie Bakeries, Inc., 365; Reid Ice Cream Corp., 241; and Beech-Nut Packing Co., 177.

An article in a 1933 issue of the *Commercial Car Journal* listed the builders of house-to-house chassis: Chevrolet, Continental-Divco, Dodge Bros., Federal, Ford, Indiana, International Harvester, Kenworth, Reo, Studebaker, Stutz, Thorne, Twin Coach, Walker, Ward, and White. Much of the article was devoted to making cost comparisons of trucks and horses. The other topic covered was the introduction of driving controls that reduced the number of separate operations that the driver had to perform.

Truck dealers had a catalog supplied by a publisher representing body builders that contained ads from the body builders who could supply and fit a body to their particular make of truck. For Chevrolet

A Ford A with an open cab used by the Forest Lawn Flower Shop in Los Angeles. *Crown Coach Corp.*

trucks, the catalog was called *The Silver Book*. The 1938 issue of that book listed the following firms as builders and suppliers of stand-up bodies that could be placed on a Chevrolet chassis: Swift Body & Equipment Co., Saginaw (whose ad showed a pie truck); The Standrive Company, Los Angeles; Metropolitan Body Co., Bridgeport, Connecticut (whose ad showed a bread truck); McCabe-Powers, St. Louis (whose ad showed a milk truck); Montpelier Manufacturing Co., Montpelier, Ohio; and Proctor-Keefe Body Co., Detroit. This was the decade when steel took the place of wood in the construction of most truck body styles.

Also during this decade, mechanical refrigeration units were being developed and very slowly adapted to use on trucks. Initially, an ice compartment was used with the amount of ice dependent upon the load and the day's anticipated temperature. Ice cream and dairy products needed to be kept cool. Some milk bodies were insulated and their light color helped reflect heat. The development of mechanical refrigeration would cut into the market for ice deliveries.

Many of the trucks pictured were used by wholesalers of "brand" names who made deliveries to retail stores. Lars Sandberg listed the foods that were distributed in the 1930s by wholesale driver/salespersons. Here's a portion of his list: bacon, baking powder, beverages, biscuits, bologna, bullion tablets, bread, butter, buttermilk, cakes, cake decorations, canned goods, cheese, coffee, coleslaw, concentrated vegetables, confectionery, cookies, cooking oil, crackers, cream, dog food, doughnuts, and dried fish. Sandberg also cited a

Donaldson's, a popular Minneapolis department store, used this 1931 Diamond-T panel on a long wheelbase. Diamond-T trucks were built in Chicago. *Allied Stores Corp.*

Six 1931 GMCs sold by a Cleveland, Ohio, dealer to the Hoover Co. for use as factory service cars. *The Hoover Co., North Canton, Ohio*

report concerning the extent of Fleischmann Yeast's distribution network: "Service is given not less than twice a week—in many cases daily—to upwards of 60,000 commercial bakeries, hotels, restaurants, public institutions, etc., and to upwards of 300,000 grocers."

The 1930s were the decade when paved roads were completed between almost all communities. This allowed trucks to be used instead of railroads for making

Ford commercial car literature for 1931 referred to this as the "Town Car Delivery." It was designed for "those shops that want striking and distinctive, yet conservative, delivery cars. The body is aluminum. Veneer panels in natural color cover the strong wooden frame of the interior. A full length sliding door connects the driver's compartment with the loading area. Equipment includes an ornamental light on either side of the body, an extension mirror on the left side, fender well for spare wheel and tire, slanting windshield, and canopy top for covering driver's compartment." *Ford Archives*

A Reading, Pennsylvania, baker used this 1931 Ward electric truck. Wards were built in Mt. Vernon, New York. *National Automotive History Collection, Detroit Public Library*

deliveries to other cities. However, the roads and their maintenance were still not up to today's standards. A Nabisco Brands company history contains this recollection of one of their drivers during that time:

> Once during a 32-inch snowfall it took me three days to haul some Chase & Sanborn coffee from Baltimore to Philadelphia. Normally that trip would have taken only four hours. My truck got stranded in a drift with a truck carrying some Bond bread, one of Fleischmann Yeast's customers. The other driver and I melted some snow, made hot coffee and lived on bread and coffee until the storm ended. Then we made our deliveries.

Wren and Wren reported these events for the decade:

1931   A survey showed that more than 75 firms were manufacturing refrigerated truck bodies.

1932   Eleven manufacturers offered "multi-stop house-to-house delivery trucks. They were: DeKalb, Divco-Detroit, Dodge, Ford, Kenworth, Step-N-Drive, Thorne, Twin Coach, Walker, Ward, and White."

1933   John A. Wanamaker's ran a fleet of 150 delivery trucks in Philadelphia. To ensure proper maintenance they began using a different color of grease each month.

1935   Ford announced that it had produced its 3 millionth truck. In 1935, the industry built 697,000 trucks.

1936   Sears trained all of its drivers in first-aid, and each of their trucks carried a first-aid kit.

1937   A power-elevator tailgate was introduced.

1938   New delivery models were introduced by Chevrolet, GMC, International, and Willys.

1940   "Standard Bread Company of Los Angeles replaced the entire company fleet of 214 delivery trucks with new White Horse 99 models. Each truck had special glass display racks for curbside selling, and musical horns that played an identifying tune." Truck production was 756,000 units, buoyed by war orders.

International introduced its "Metro" body, using a design that would last until 1965. Fred Crismon wrote in *International Trucks*: "The new Metro was a very attractive design. It was smooth, with no projecting fenders or corners, and generally resembled a short loaf of bread. The large, flat sides and rear offered an abundance of advertising space. It even came with fender skirts on the originals which helped give it a finished appearance."

The 75th anniversary issue of the *Commercial Carrier Journal* listed these developments during the decade: the diesel engine, use of aluminum in bodies, two-speed rear axles, synchromesh transmissions, and mechanical refrigeration units for trucks.

In 1935, Marshall Field's retired the last electric truck from its fleet. In their system, all packages left the main store by large trailers which were taken to a delivery station where the packages were sorted by route. On a record day before Christmas, their system handled more than 103,000 packages.

An early-1930s International panel on a long wheelbase used to distribute ice cream. *Navistar Archives*

United States Plywood Company ran this ad in a 1932 truck body builders' trade magazine advertising a coated plywood that was used in milk delivery bodies. The truck shown is a 1932 Ward Electric, one of a fleet of 64 built for Borden's by the York-Hoover Body Co. of York, Pennsylvania. *American Automobile Manufacturers Association*

A 1932 Dodge used by a Hoover vacuum dealer for sales and service calls. Painted on the cowl in small lettering are the truck's weight, capacity, and tire size. The first two measures were often used for licensing purposes, but the reason for painting the tire size is unknown. *The Hoover Co., North Canton, Ohio*

These Mack Bulldogs distributed cigarettes. Note the emblem on the cab doors saying "BABACO Alarm System." If the alarm was set, it would sound if someone attempted to break into the truck or move it. Early BABACO literature appeared to be aimed at dry cleaners who specialized in cleaning and storing furs. *Babaco*

This 1933 Indiana coal truck's body is elevated with a hydraulic hoist so that coal will flow down a slide-like device into the customer's basement. Indiana trucks were associated with White trucks. *Volvo/White*

A 1932 Mack used to deliver
Ben-Hur coffee. *Mack Museum*

These small 1933 Internationals were actually produced by Willys-Overland. This one has a fancy body, including landau lights. Note the laundry driver's outfit. *Navistar Archives*

A 1933 Indiana used by a Philco radio distributor. *Volvo/White*

Three 1933 Kenworths with step-van bodies used to deliver Carnation milk. Carnation had initially sold condensed milk through grocery stores but then began buying dairies and distributing fresh milk. *Kenworth Truck Company*

Marshall Field & Company used this 1934 International with body built by General Body Co. The body is higher than a conventional panel body. *General Body Company, Chicago*

The Mayer Body Corporation of Pittsburgh built this milk body and placed it on a 1934 Dodge chassis. Original information mimeographed on the back of the photo said: "Special retail milk delivery body. Body 96" long, 42" wide, 52" high, inside. Cases arranged three cases wide, four cases high, five cases long, total sixty case capacity. Doors at the rear are to have offset hinges permitting the rear doors to fold and lock against the sides." *Mayer*

A 1934 White panel truck with Ohio plates delivering newspapers. *Volvo/White*

Twin Coach, located in Lima, Ohio, built mainly buses but they also produced some stand-up vans in the first half of the 1930s. *Carnation*

American Body & Equipment Co. of Dallas built this mechanically-cooled ice-cream body to be carried on a mid-1930s Dodge. *American Body & Equipment Co.*

UPS used this 1934 White step-van. *Volvo/White*

A custom front end was put on this mid-1930s GMC, used for the delivery of ice cream. *A. L. Hansen Mfg. Co.*

A mid-1930s International panel used by a "music house." At rear, an upright radio is about to be loaded. *Navistar Archives*

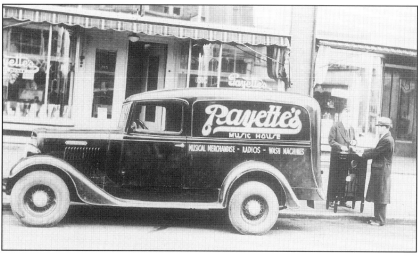

A mid-1930s International panel truck delivering Hormel products to a retail grocer in Boston. *Hormel*

A mid-1930s Indiana with an insulated body used by a dairy. Note the racks inside. *Columbia Body & Equipment Co.*

This is a 1935 International chassis and the design would lead to later step-van models. This truck was used by a bakery. *Navistar Archives*

A view into the back shows drawers for storing bakery products. *Navistar Archives*

W. Everett Miller was a Southern California auto and truck body designer whose name is usually associated with custom limousines and sports cars. He did some work with streamlining fire apparatus and truck bodies. This is one of his sketches of a food vendor's body. *Blackhawk Classic Auto Collection*

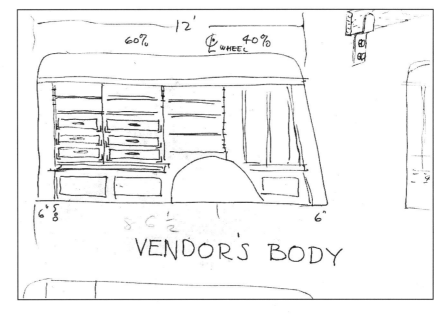

This 1935 Stewart had a streamlined body and was used for delivering Edelbrau beer. Stewarts were built in Buffalo. *National Automotive History Collection, Detroit Public Library*

This is a 1935 Terraplane. Taxicabs must be included when writing about deliveries within cities since they were often used to make deliveries. While local regulations differed, some drivers would have permanent relationships with certain merchants and perform deliveries at regular fares. Or, they would put the package in their trunk and deliver it when they happened to be near its destination. *American Automobile Manufacturers Association*

"Good Humor" trucks went to parks and into neighborhoods during summer months to peddle ice cream. These trucks are 1936 Chevrolets. *Baker Library, Harvard University*

This 1935 White Model 701 was used by McKelvey's, a store in Youngstown, Ohio. *Volvo/White*

McCabe-Powers built this high body for use by a florist. Note the rack above the cab roof. The chassis is a 1936–37 Diamond-T. *McCabe-Powers Body Co.*

A fleet consisting mainly of 1936 Chevrolets used by the Coca-Cola Bottling Co. in Vernon, Texas. The truck in the foreground is used for sales and promotional purposes; the others make deliveries to retailers. Each of the trucks in the background appears to have a single high cooler. Those probably carried iced Coca-Cola for immediate sale. *Coca-Cola*

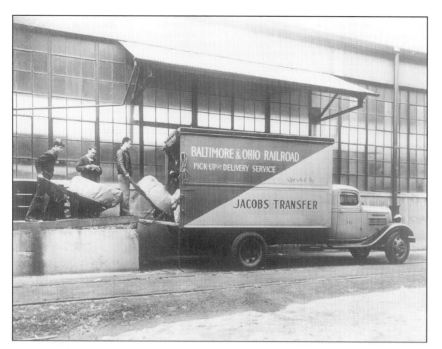

Railway Express Agency freight moved on passenger trains. Freight trains also carried small items of freight, called "LCL" (for less-than-carload). Railroads also offered pickup and delivery service for this freight, which is how the Baltimore and Ohio Railroad used this 1936 GMC. Jacobs Transfer had the local franchise for handling this service in the city where the picture was taken. *Smithsonian Institution*

Several styles of delivery bodies were shown on Dodge chassis at a 1936 truck show. In the center is a commercial panel used by a dairy, with a sign in the license plate bracket indicating that it sold for $595. In the background, from the left, we see trucks that carried gasoline, bread, and beer. *Chrysler Historical Collection*

A 1936 Mack Jr. with a stand-up milk delivery body. *National Automotive History Collection, Detroit Public Library*

A fleet of 1936 Mack Jrs. with step-van bodies, used by Sears. *California State Archives*

The Pennsylvania Railroad used this 1936 Studebaker for door-to-door deliveries of LCL rail freight. In 1936, U.S. railroads used over 33,000 trucks for delivering to stores; and this was in addition to the 10,000+ trucks used by the Railway Express Agency. *Smithsonian Institution*

In the period from about 1935 to 1940, slip-on pickup boxes were sold that fit into the trunk spaces of popular makes of autos. They could be removed when not needed. This one is shown mounted on a 1936 Terraplane. *Baker Library, Harvard University*

A Hackney stand-up body on a 1937
Dodge chassis. *Hackney Bros. Body Co.*

American Bantam offered this panel in the late 1930s. This pair was used for vending ice cream. The Bantam firm was best know for
developing the Jeep. *Mike Margerum*

This is a "Standrive-Chevrolet" built in the late 1930s by the Standrive Company, using a Chevrolet chassis. *American Automobile Manufacturers Association*

Here's a cutaway drawing of the Standrive-Chevrolet. *The William F. Harrah Automobile Foundation*

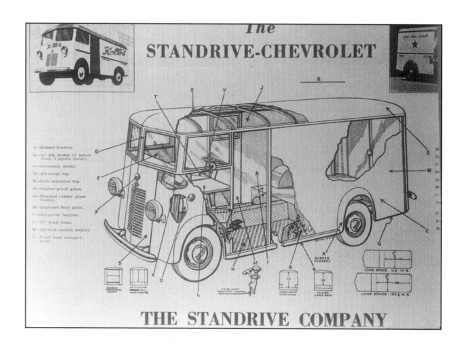

Note how bread is stored in the high body of this late-1930s International. There is also a side door toward the front of the body. *Navistar Archives*

A 1937 International with a plate-glass-carrying body used by Fuller. The truck had a 184-inch wheelbase and its carry rack was 8x11 feet. *Navistar Archives*

A late-1930s International panel truck used by a canteen company that distributed and serviced vending machines. *Navistar Archives*

Spare vending machines and coin boxes are strapped inside the rear. *Navistar Archives*

A circa-1937 Mack Jr. used by a meat market. *American Truck Historical Society*

Marmon-Herrington built these trucks used by Langendorf Bakeries. The front of the body below the windshield would pull out to allow servicing or replacing the engine. Marmon-Herrington, of Indianapolis, was best know for its all-wheel-drive conversion kits for Ford products. *Crown Coach Corp.*

This W. Everett Miller sketch shows the side of a fancy delivery truck intended for Bullock's, a Southern California department store. *Blackhawk Classic Auto Collection*

A 1937 Chevrolet with a Hackney stand-up milk body. *Hackney Bros. Body Co.*

A Wentworth & Irwin stand-up milk body on a late-1930s GMC chassis. *Columbia Body & Equipment Co.*

A 1936 Dodge with a custom panel body, and two 1938 Divcos. All were part of a dairy's fleet. *Beatrice Foods*

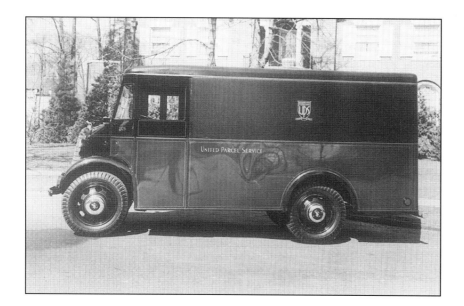

A late-1930s Mack Jr. with a stand-up body used by United Parcel Service. *UPS*

The Wilton Farm Dairy of Catonsville, Maryland, had a mural entitled "our farm" on the side of its truck, a late-1930s Mack. A second sign said "city wide delivery," although this size of truck was probably used to make deliveries to retail outlets. *American Automobile Manufacturers Association*

This toy truck, probably based on a late-1930s International, commemorates Classic Motorbooks' 20th anniversary. The firm is now MBI Publishing Company.

This is a step-van body, circa 1938, built by Metro Body Co. of Bridgeport, Connecticut. It's probably on an International chassis. Later, International would buy this firm, making it a subsidiary. The wording at the bottom of the picture says "Doubles Payload Capacity of Light Duty Trucks." *National Automotive History Collection, Detroit Public Library*

General Body Co. of Chicago used a late-1930s White chassis to build this fancy florists' body. The rear window panel, which showed a floral display, would be changed seasonally. *A. L. Hansen Mfg. Co.*

There are 1938 Texas plates on what must be a truck for carrying pies. *Texas DOT*

A late-1930s Autocar COE with a refrigerated body used by Safeway to deliver meat to its retail stores. *Eight-Point Trailer Corp., Los Angeles*

A late-1930s Dodge chassis was used by Gillig to build this milk delivery body for a dairy in Woodland, California, currently home of the Hays Antique Truck Museum. *Gillig Corp.*

Dodge and International panel trucks from the late 1930s deliver Meadow Gold Dairy products. *Beatrice Foods*

Bookmobiles are similar to traveling stores in that they make scheduled stops where clients are waiting. This 1939 GMC has stopped in front of a school. Open display shelves line either side, and the center of the body is raised with an aisle going down the center to give access to shelves running the length of the truck body. *American Automobile Manufacturers Association*

General Body Company of Chicago built this stand-up van in the late 1930s. It looks similar to Internationals of that era. *General Body Company, Chicago*

A 1939 GMC flatbed used by a lumber company in McDonough, New York, to deliver pre-assembled portions of a new house to a building site. *American Automobile Manufacturers Association*

A late-1930s International cab-over, used by a New York furniture dealer. Furniture to be delivered has been wrapped in heavy padding.

The Michigan State Library used a step-van for a three-sheet fold-up table display, advertising its bookmobile and other services. *American Library Association*

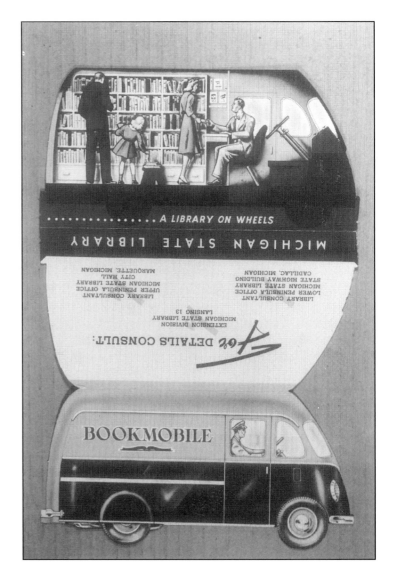

A Hackney soft-drink body on a 1940 Chevrolet chassis used to distribute Dr. Pepper. *Hackney Bros. Body Co.*

The Few Acres Dairy near San Diego used this 1939 White Horse. *Volvo/White*

A small delivery truck was offered by Crosley in 1940. The wheelbase was 80 inches and the engine delivered 12 horsepower. *American Automobile Manufacturers Association*

Young Electric Sign Co. of Salt Lake City used these trucks for installing and servicing signs. The truck in the foreground is a 1940 Chevrolet sedan delivery. Behind it are some slightly older Studebakers. *Young Electric Sign Co.*

Two views of a 1940 Diamond-T "Pak-Age-Car". *Mike Pagel*

This cutaway drawing shows how milk cases would be stored. In front near the driver is an iced compartment that holds four cases. *Mike Pagel*

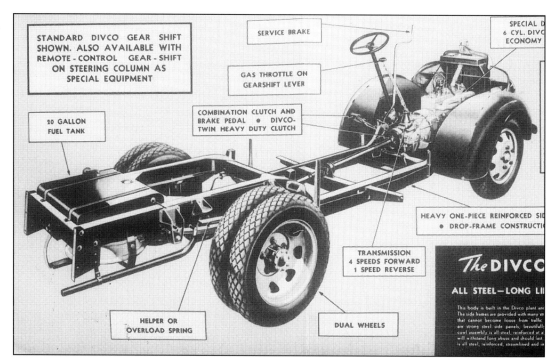

The chassis of a Divco. Controls differ from a conventional truck's. The service brake handle sticks up in the air like a tiller; the gas throttle is on the gearshift lever; and there is a combination clutch and brake pedal. A note in the upper left indicates that it's "also available with remote-control gear-shift on steering column."

This photo shows a range of small delivery bodies used during the 1930s. The truck in front is a wooden stand-up body on a Ford A chassis. After that is a 1936 Dodge panel (sometimes called a "humpback" because of its higher truck compartment). Next is a 1936 panel, then a step-van, and at the far end a 1940 White Horse. *Volvo/White*

The Schnable Company of Pittsburgh built this demonstrator stand-up bread body on a 1940 Ford light-truck chassis. *Historical Society of Western Pennsylvania*

Signs on top of trucks were used on routes near apartment buildings. This truck is a late-1930s International Metro. *Navistar Archives*

Prior to mechanical refrigeration, ice was used to cool railcars carrying perishables. This photo, taken in Milwaukee in 1940, shows an International with a hydraulic scissors-lift, elevating a platform so the ice could be placed in the ice compartments of the railcar. *Navistar Archives*

Kiel Bottling Works, Kiel, Wisconsin, owned this 1940 Ford 3/4-ton panel for many years. The emblem on the front fenders looks like a giant bottle top.
Michael J. Kissinger

This 1940 photo shows a downtown street in Ontario, Oregon. A step-van, operated by a laundry called "Rain Water Jones," is double-parked, not uncommon for delivery trucks.

Walker Electric trucks were made until 1942, and their appearance changed very little over the years. This one was used by Bowman Dairy and painted dark, which was unusual for a milk truck. It's shown during World War II when it carried signs promoting war bonds. *American Truck Historical Society*

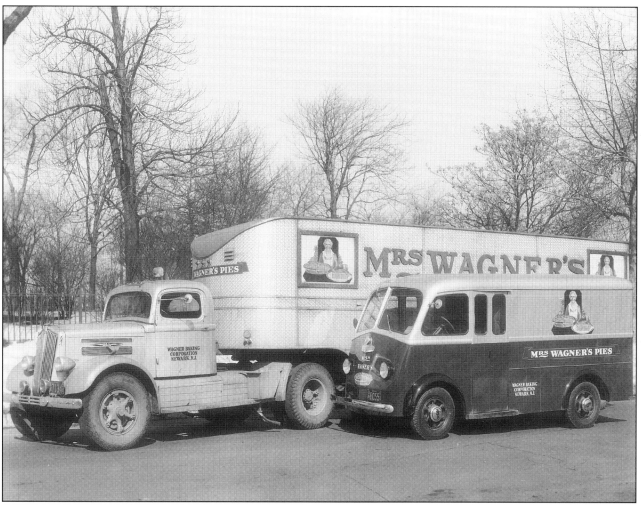

Two different sizes of 1940 White trucks used for distributing Mrs. Wagner's Pies. The small truck made deliveries to retailers while the large truck either made deliveries to wholesalers or brought pies from some distance where they were loaded onto the smaller trucks. *Volvo/White*

Chapter Five

1941–1950

During the first half of the 1940s, the nation was involved in World War II. Shortages of gasoline and tires prolonged the use of horses for making deliveries. In a few trades, such as beer distribution, the use of horses increased. Some truck body builders actually built new horse-drawn delivery wagons for civilian use. Some delivery routes were also shortened. "During the war, I helped cut down the length of delivery routes. We had to conserve gasoline," a driver was quoted as saying in the Nabisco Brands company history.

At the war's end there began a "rush" to the suburbs, which changed shopping patterns. Nearly all suburban dwellers had access to autos, and as shopping centers sprung up, they were designed for customers with autos. A dry cleaning business, for example, could establish a dry cleaning outlet in a suburban mall without offering home pickup and delivery service. Suburban department stores, too, offered fewer delivery services than did their downtown stores.

There is no end to the number of statistics that one might cite to demonstrate the increase in ownership of autos. The one we will use comes from the American Automobile Manufacturers Association. They reported that 1948 registrations were 30 million autos and 6.6 million trucks, totalling 36.6 million motor vehicles. (Comparable 1997 figures were 125 million autos and 76 million trucks, totalling 201 million vehicles. There are more licensed vehicles today than there are licensed drivers! In the figures just given, note that truck numbers are growing faster than autos; that's because the vast majority of trucks sold are small pickups or vans, used solely for personal transportation.)

Wren and Wren noted some of the following events during the decade:

1941 Crosley introduced several models of 1/4-ton trucks.

1942 Tires and gasoline were rationed, and sales of new trucks for commercial uses were highly restricted.

1944 Late in the year, the War Production Board authorized the manufacture of light civilian trucks.

1945 Truck and trailer rationing ended on December 1, 1945. Marmon-Herrington announced a door-to-door van, the "Delivr-all."

1946 Vanette, Incorporated, a Detroit-based company, announced three delivery models available on Ford chassis, and Reynolds Metal offered "knocked-down" van bodies that two people could assemble. Assembled, they were 7 feet wide, 6 feet high, and lengths ranged from 10 to 14 feet.

1948 Dodge introduced a line of route vans.

1949 Ford introduced a parcel delivery chassis with optional air brakes.

1950 International introduced two refrigerated trucks for multi-stop deliveries. Truck and bus production had climbed to 1,377,000 units.

The American Automobile Manufacturers Association listed the largest private truck fleets in 1948, and did so by industry. The bakery list had 21 names with General Baking Company having the largest fleet (4,534) and Braun Baking Co. the smallest (142). Nineteen other food companies were listed. Of these, Jewel Tea had the largest truck fleet (1,953) and H. C. Bohack the smallest (80). Five meat packers were listed with Swift & Co. having the largest fleet (3,200) and John Morrell & Co. the smallest (146). National Dairy Products led the dairy industry (10,000 trucks), and Metzger Dairies was 13th and last on the dairy list (106 trucks).

The *Chicago Herald American* had a delivery fleet of 230 trucks. Seventeen other newspapers were listed and the one with the smallest fleet (53) was the *Cleveland Press*. Very large fleets were reported for the petroleum industry and for public utilities. A few others we will mention are Firestone (1,684); R. J. Reynolds Tobacco (721); Railway Express Agency (15,000); United Parcel Service (4,069); Brink's (825); City Ice & Fuel (2,000); Sears (748); Consolidated Laundries (583); and Marshall Field's (278). All figures given are for straight trucks; there were separate categories for semi-tractors, trailers, and autos.

Millington Truck Body Company of Millington, Michigan, offered a standard "Merchandiser" body and then offered different kinds of shelving to be placed inside to adapt it to different kinds of customers. Their eight styles of shelving were designed to accommodate groceries, with built-in cooler for butter and ice cream; bread, cakes, and pastries; fruits and vegetables; bottles; cigars and tobacco; maintenance and service; plumbing and tool storage; and auto parts. Literature from the Stewart Truck Bodies firm of Brooklyn offered these options for their medium-size panel truck body: double doors above tailgate; full double doors to swing around sides (needed to back up with the doors open);

curtain above tailgate; folding chain gate; hydraulic lift tailgate; rear wheelhousings (either square or round); tie knobs; recessed tie hooks; side doors; dome lights; directional lights; courtesy lights; reflectors; rear bumper; and tool box.

In 1948, International Harvester purchased the Metropolitan Body Works of Bridgeport—the outfitter of its "Metro" bodies—and made it a subsidiary. Some Metro bodies were adapted to passenger-carrying uses.

A Blue Bell potato chips distributor in Everett, Washington, used this 1941 Chevrolet with a Heiser body. There is a side door by the word "Bell" and a step below it. *Geo. Heiser Body Co.*

An attractive 1941 Chevrolet sedan delivery. After World War II, sedan deliveries would become less popular, with one reason being that the lower height of the body made them less useful for hauling cargo. *Chevrolet*

A 1941 Dodge panel truck operated by a diaper service in New York City. Note the rack on the roof for holding soiled diapers that have been picked up. *American Automobile Manufacturers Association*

An early-1940s Dodge stake truck used for carrying gas cylinders. Chains and cables are used to keep cylinders in upright positions. *Press Tank & Equipment Co., Chicago*

A small 1941 Ford pickup used for delivering ice. Barely visible behind the rear fender is a machine for chopping blocks of ice into chips. *Central Power & Light, Corpus Christi*

Three early-1940s GMCs used by the Kaaser's bakery. *Fred A. Albrecht Grocery Co.*

The Pittsburgh Press was distributed in this early-1940s Dodge. Note that the body had more cube than a conventional panel truck. *Historical Society of Western Pennsylvania*

This Mack with a van body was called the "Mack Retailer" and was sold between 1940 and 1942. *Mack Museum*

A Champaign, Illinois, liquor dealer used this 1941 Reo with a McCabe-Powers Body. *McCabe-Powers Body Co.*

A 1941 Walker Electric used by UPS. *UPS*

A 1942 Ford with an open, covered milk body, used by Borden's in the suburbs south of San Francisco. It probably made deliveries to retail or institutional customers. *San Mateo Historical Museum*

Horses were used for home deliveries way beyond the 1940s, with World War II probably extending their years of usefulness. Note that this bread rig has rubber tires. The boy is coaxing the horse to venture where it shouldn't. A sugar cube is the likely attraction. Freihofer's horse deliveries lasted until 1962. *Freihofer*

This horse-drawn milk wagon was built in 1942. It has rubber tires. *Murphy Mfg. Co.*

A World War II–era Mack (with no chrome) carrying a stand-up milk body. *Mack Museum*

A small World War II emblem on the door of a 1940 Ford panel indicates a patriotic pledge that Kiel Bottling Works made regarding truck use. *Michael J. Kissinger*

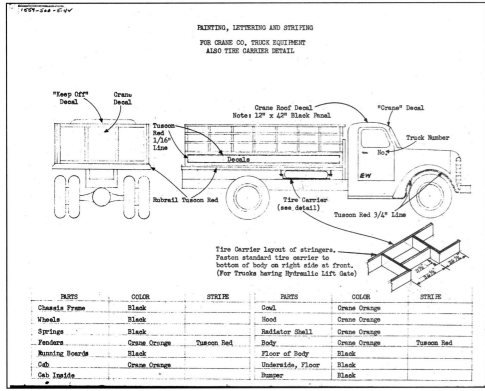

PAINTING, LETTERING AND STRIPING

FOR CRANE CO. TRUCK EQUIPMENT
ALSO TIRE CARRIER DETAIL

"Keep Off" Decal
Crane Decal
Crane Roof Decal
Note: 12" x 42" Black Panel
"Crane" Decal
Tuscon Red 1/16" Line
Truck Number
No.
Decals
EW
Rubrail Tuscon Red
Tire Carrier (see detail)
Tuscon Red 3/4" Line

Tire Carrier layout of stringers.
Fasten standard tire carrier to bottom of body on right side at front.
(For Trucks having Hydraulic Lift Gate)

PARTS	COLOR	STRIPE	PARTS	COLOR	STRIPE
Chassis Frame	Black		Cowl	Crane Orange	
Wheels	Black		Hood	Crane Orange	
Springs	Black		Radiator Shell	Crane Orange	
Fenders	Crane Orange	Tuscon Red	Body	Crane Orange	Tuscon Red
Running Boards	Black		Floor of Body	Black	
Cab	Crane Orange		Underside, Floor	Black	
Cab Inside	Black		Bumper	Black	

Firms that operated fleets of trucks often wished to have them painted uniformly to reinforce the firm's image. Here is a fleet painting chart used by The Crane Company, indicating paint colors and placement of decals. *The Crane Co.*

This early-1940s Diamond-T is carrying a body that is raised with two telescopic hoists. It was built by the Hockensmith Corporation and was delivered to an ice company that probably used it for icing railroad cars. Similar hoists are used today by roofing companies and for loading/unloading aircraft. *John C. Steighner*

Sky Chief, Inc. used this 1945 White Horse to deliver prepared meals to an American Airlines DC-3 in Boston. *Volvo/White*

Available trucks were built in Chicago from 1910 until 1957. This 1946 Available has a coal body that was built and installed by Auto Truck Equipment Sales of Chicago. *Auto Truck*

Placing Divco bodies on chassis, circa 1946. This style of Divco had been introduced in 1938 and lasted nearly 50 years. *American Automobile Manufacturers Association*

A Reliance furniture body on a 1940s Ford COE for use by a San Francisco furniture store. *Dailey Body Co.*

A tire distributor had this body built on a mid-1940s Ford chassis. *Geo. Heiser Body Co.*

Two 1946 GMCs and a 1946 Chevrolet sedan delivery used by Meadow Gold Dairy. The sedan delivery was used by a salesperson. *Beatrice Foods*

The body on this mid-1940s International is short but has racks inside for carrying plate glass. It was used in the Pacific Northwest. *Geo. Heiser Body Co.*

A mid-1940s Studebaker that distributed frozen foods, operating out of Holdredge, Nebraska. Many farmers had their own freezers and were a market for types of frozen food they didn't grow. *General Body Company, Chicago*

A 1947 Dodge delivering Puritas bottled water to an I. Magnin store in Southern California. *Arrowhead*

View over the shoulder of a milkman in a conventional panel truck. To his right, above the glove compartment, is a ringed binder with a separate sheet to record deliveries to each customer. *Library of Congress*

A cigar-tobacco-candy wholesaler with operations in both Cheyenne, Wyoming, and Sidney, Nebraska, used this 1947 International with a Timpte body. The body hardware makes it look like it's insulated, or at least, sealed. *Timpte, Inc.*

This is a 1947 White Horse, built by White. Note horse's-head hood ornament. *Volvo/White*

For a few years after World War II, Marmon-Herrington built a step-van they called the "Delivr-all." *Blackhawk Classic Auto Collection*

A toy company in Seattle had this Heiser body placed on a late-1940s Chevrolet chassis. *Geo. Heiser Body Co.*

This is a 1948 Diamond-T, used by Jordan Marsh, a large Boston department store. *Allied Stores Corp.*

This Divco's sturdy roof held in this roll-over accident. *Steve Ritchie*

A Grumman/Olson demonstrator body on a GMC chassis, circa 1947–1949. *Grumman/Olson*

This is a food-vending body built by Grumman/Olson in the later 1940s. These trucks would often go on regular routes supplying workers with snacks and lunches. *Grumman/Olson*

A late-1940s International Metro body outfitted and painted by the Heiser Co. of Seattle. *Geo. Heiser Body Co.*

A 1948 Studebaker auto chassis to which a step-van body has been added. Perhaps this was originally an auto and the rear end of the body was wrecked beyond repair while the front half was unscratched, so a new body was built at the rear. *Mike Margerum*

A UPS truck built by Grumman/Olson in the late 1940s. The chassis is probably a Chevrolet. *Grumman/Olson*

New White trucks on display in 1948. The center truck is a White Horse stand-up van, to be used by Sealtest. At right is a model 3000 that will be used by Borden's. *Volvo/White*

A late-1940s Willys Jeep panel delivery. *National Archives*

A late-1940s Chevrolet long-wheelbase panel that carried Curtis candy.

A loading area for parcels to be delivered from a Block's department store in Indianapolis, circa 1949. *Allied Stores Corp.*

Abbey Rents had a Heiser body placed on a late-1940s Chevrolet COE chassis. *Geo. Heiser Body Co.*

A Hesse stand-up body on a late-1940s Chevrolet. *Hesse Corporation*

A Seattle ice-cream wholesaler had this Heiser refrigerated body placed on a late-1940s Chevrolet COE chassis. *Geo. Heiser Body Co.*

A Chicago plumber used this 1949 International Metro which has a grille guard and outside racks for holding pipes. *Navistar Archives*

There's also a pipe storage area below the truck's floor. *Navistar Archives*

This picture was taken at the end of the Grumman/Olson assembly line in the late 1940s. *Grumman/Olson*

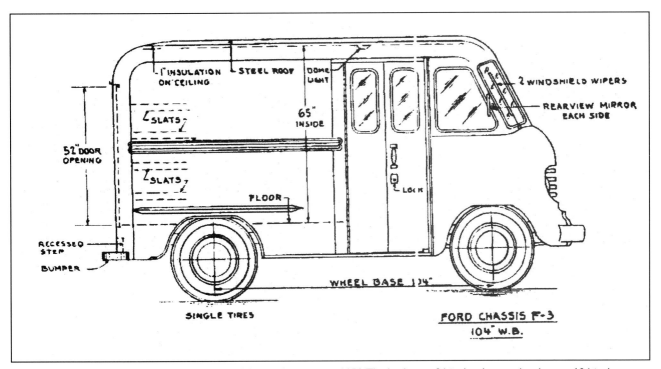

A Herman body intended for a Ford F-3 parcel delivery chassis, circa 1950. The body was 96 inches long and rode on a 104-inch wheelbase. A body 120 inches long could ride on an F-3 122-inch wheelbase. A body 144 inches long was designed to fit on a Ford F-5 with a 134-inch wheelbase. *Herman Body Co.*

Chapter Six

1951–1960

The 1950s began with the Korean War. In economic terms it was a very prosperous decade, and there was growth in the suburbs and in highway transportation. The Interstate Highway System was begun, which doubled the truck's competitive range, compared with the railroad.

A development arose at this time that has remained a factor throughout the postwar decades: the rise of large retail chains that depend upon single, central sources of supply. This development changed the patterns of deliveries and the character of trucks used to perform them. We'll cite two examples: McDonald's and 7-Eleven. McDonald's outlets are supplied by a single firm, Martin-Brower (known today as a logistics services provider). Their semi-trailers make single deliveries to each outlet of all the food and other supplies, such as napkins and straws, the outlet is projected to need until the next scheduled delivery. This can be contrasted to an independent restaurant that would receive small quantities of goods delivered in separate trucks. Meat, fish, produce, dry groceries, baked goods, and restaurant supplies would each arrive on a different truck. The patterns for 7-Elevens are the same; they are also served through a single warehouse, unlike small "Mom and Pop" grocery stores that receive merchandise from ten or so different suppliers.

A fleet-painting manual from about 1950 was found in the ARCO files, 18 pages long, and dealing with the painting of "Richfield" petroleum trucks. The manual covered both the painting of new trucks and the repainting of old trucks to conform with the new scheme. (On older trucks, for example, chrome was to be carefully inspected and, if in poor shape, sanded and painted.)

Lettering instructions included requirements to meet the company's internal or legal needs, such as painting the capacity of each tank. Various state requirements for lettering were listed, including an indication of the vehicle's weight, and the size and placement of the words "gasoline" or "fuel oil." There was a two-page chart listing the quantities needed of colored paints, primers, surfacers, and stencil adhesive, by size of truck. Two of the colors, "Richfield Blue" and "Richfield Yellow" had to be obtained from the company. Other materials could be obtained from Fuller paint dealers. Decals showing the Richfield eagle were available from the company, as were stencil masks needed for lettering. Because of the different truck sizes involved, it was necessary to have different instructions for each size.

Several pages were devoted to showing three views—front, rear, and side—of each style and size of truck to be painted. Finally, a sheet was included describing how to obtain bids from local paint shops. The bidder had to specify that he would "furnish all labor, equipment and materials necessary (except stenciling masks, decals, and blue and yellow paint) to steam clean, paint and letter in Richfield colors in accordance with Richfield painting specifications."

For this decade, Wren and Wren reports these events:

1951 There was experimentation using propane and LNG as fuel.

1952 Short-haul transportation of mail was switched from rail to truck.

1953 Automatic transmissions became available for most light trucks.

1954 Willys developed a right-hand steering vehicle for mail delivery.

1955 New truck and bus production totalled 1,254,000 units.

1956 Tubeless tires for trucks came into use.

1957 Chevrolet introduced two new multi-stop delivery chassis to be outfitted by body builders, and Dodge introduced a "stand-

A 1951 Autocar used by a Long Island coal dealer. It has 12 compartments that each holds one ton, making it possible to make individual deliveries. Note that each compartment has its own chute opening. A small sign on the frame says: "Guaranteed Net Weight, Coal Consumers Protective Association." Above that are some blank slots and the abbreviation "lbs." The truck's empty weight was probably printed there. A weight inspector could stop the loaded coal truck as it was leaving a coal yard and ask for documentation indicating how much coal they were delivering. Say, for example, the documents showed that they were about to deliver (and collect payment for) nine tons of coal. The inspector would then have the truck go to a public scale, where its weight should equal the net empty weight shown on the side of the truck, plus nine tons. *Volvo/White*

drive" model with a 95-inch wheelbase. Truck safes were devised for driver/salespersons who were to deposit immediately most of their collections into a slot that fed into the safe which was attached to the truck and could only be opened at the terminal.

1958 Considerable efforts were made to substitute lightweight metals for steel in trucks in order to reduce weights.

1960 Hazard lamps were required. Truck and bus production was at 1,202,000 units.

According to the *Commercial Carrier Journal's* 75th anniversary issue, notable developments during the decade included gas-turbine engines, air suspension, tubeless tires, transistorized ignition systems, and the use of fiberglass for hoods and body parts.

Toward the end of this decade "sedan deliveries" offered on full-size auto chassis were discontinued. The principal reason was that auto styling had resulted in roofs so low that there was relatively little room for cargo. Later, some compacts would offer a sedan delivery equivalent as did many van bodies.

An early-1950s long-wheelbase Chevrolet panel used by the Canadian Pacific Express to pick up and deliver small parcels that moved intercity by rail. *Canadian Pacific Corporation Corporate Archives Collection*

An early-1950s International Metro used by Goodyear. The rack on top holds extra tires. *American Automobile Manufacturers Association*

An early-1950s Studebaker used to deliver Quaker State packaged products to service stations. *Geo. Heiser Body Co.*

Trucks with refrigerated and freezer bodies often could "plug in" to keep their cargo space cold while parked overnight. *Autac, Inc.*

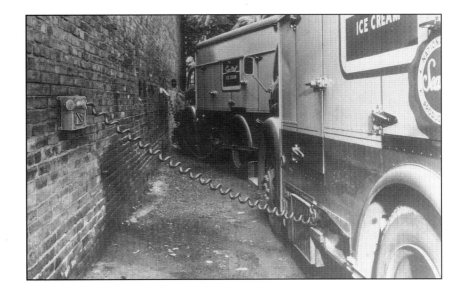

A Hewitt-Lucas milk body on a 1952 Ford chassis. *Hewitt-Lucas Body Co.*

Hood's Dairy of Boston had both a restored Divco and a battery-powered child-size model.

An early-1950s White cab-over used by a Brooklyn distributor of Schaefer beer. Note the large compartments on the side of the Gerstenslager-built body. They are for holding pallets of beer, which would be loaded and unloaded by fork-lift trucks. A truck like this made deliveries to large customers who dealt in pallet-loads of product. *Gerstenslager Corp.*

Powered tailgates came into widespread use after World War II. Prior to the war, when labor was much cheaper, a second man would often ride along to help handle the cargo or carry it between the truck and the customer while the driver stayed with the truck. After the war, the helper became too expensive, so devices like this powered tailgate, shown with two cans of milk, came into use. *Historical Society of Western Pennsylvania*

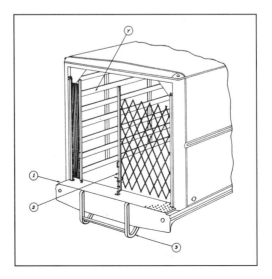

Trucks making deliveries in urban areas often had collapsible rear gates which—in some areas—were kept locked. Other features listed in an excerpt of Timpte Bros. literature were slotted wood lining inside the truck body, and bumperette and rear step. *Timpte, Inc.*

Twin Coach built some moving vans and this 1953-model truck was used for carrying meat. *American Automobile Manufacturers Association*

Carnation milk was delivered in the Heiser stand-up body mounted on a 1954 GMC chassis. *Geo. Heiser Body Co.*

Sears used this mid-1950s International. Small lettering under the door says "Pittsburgh Deliveries, Inc.," which probably owned and operated the truck under a contract with Sears. A Pennsylvania Public Utilities Commission permit number is also given, meaning that the truck's rates and services were somewhat regulated by the state. *Thiele, Inc.*

Two thicknesses of plywood are used for strength and insulation on this dairy body being built by Heiser. *Geo. Heiser Body Co.*

This is a worksheet used to help a milkman determine the profitability of his operation. A supervisor, carrying a stopwatch, would accompany him on his route. The "mark up book" activity mentioned in the lower right was used by the driver to record the amount of each delivery for billing purposes. (The form has been shortened in the center.)

```
AM Starting Time, Load a/o Unload        Time  4:10   Salesman  _____
Starting Mileage (at plant)        568   Time  4:15   Route #  9
Mileage at First Stop              569   Time  4:18   Super.  Alan B
Mileage at Last Stop               590   Time 11:45
Ending Mileage (at plant)          573   Time 11:54
PM Ending Time, Load a/o Unload  45 min  Time 12:41
Check In (Finish Day)            12 min  Time 12:56
                        Total Time:  Hours 8   Minutes 46
```

	Front Porch	Back Porch	Inside or Ask	Solicitations
Time 1st hour: 5:18	45 35 30 / 55 30 35	85 / 75		Hour 6th Time :51 / Hour 6th Time 5:09 / Hour 6th Time 1:01
Miles 1st hour: 574	90 110 120 / 63 55 34	85 / 103	None	Hour___ Time___
Dollars Sold: 30.31 ave 1.13	88 35 / 50 55	50		Hour___ Time___
Accounts Served: 20 15 10	45 51 / 45 30			Hour___ Time___
Time 2nd hour: 6:18	20 35 42 30 / 23 81 38 30	75 / 120		Collections from Customers not receiving delivery:
Miles 2nd hour: 577	35 60 28 50 / 30 30 25 70	60 / 61	None	Hour 2nd Time 3 0 / Hour 7th Time 33
Dollars Sold: 75 ave 1.11	182 38 48 60 / 30 108 70	60		Hour___ Time___
Accounts Served: 22 15 10	23 64 82 / 45 44 37			Hour___ Time___
Time 3rd hour: 7:18	20 30 40 / 25 38 23		120	Hour___ Time___
Miles 3rd hour: 580	42 41 / 55 41			Hour___ Time___
Dollars Sold: 33 ave 1.83	70 28 / 92 65	None		TOTAL → 3 39
Accounts Served: 18 1 9 11	22 45	53 56 120 55 50 60 35	85 195 / 128 240 / 95 98 97 120 60	Rest/Eating Stops: Hour 3rd Time 20 0 / Hour 4th Time 11 8 / Hour 7th Time 21 4
Time ___	44 30 17 20 27			Hour___ Time___
Dollars Sold: 31 ave 1.00				Hour___ Time___
Accounts Served: 10 7 9				TOTAL → 58 min 12 sec
Time 6th hour: 10:18	20 31 10 75 55 58 30	73 73 90 45 75 75 126 117	170 110 85 60 180 120 120 126	REMARKS: MARK UP BOOK 1st. 7.00 / " " " 2nd 5.20 / " " " 3rd 3:00 / " " " 4th 4:00 / STRAIGHTEN TRUCK OUT 6.00 / MARK UP BOOK 6th 3:50
Miles 6th hour: 586				TOTAL → 28 min 50 sec
Dollars Sold: 74.01 ave 1.48				
Accounts Served: 7 18 18				
c 7th hour: 11:18	30 48 23 47 42	65 60 63 40	77 240 97 85 90	BROKED UP 2 TIMES BECAUSE OF DEAD END STREET TOOK 2 30 SEC
Miles 7th hour: 589				DELIVERIES 170
Dollars Sold: 14.49 ave 1.04				DOLLAR SALES 191.53
Accounts Served: 5 1 4 15				COMMISSION 32.92 / SALES PER STOP 1.13

A mid-1950s productmobile looking like two milk cartons, built on a mid-1950s Dodge. *General Body Company, Chicago*

This form was used by the milkman's supervisor to help the milkman determine the "profitability" of each customer. The sales volume per customer is shown across the top and the number of deliveries the customer received was recorded along the side. (Customers could receive varying levels of service, from stops every other day to only once a week.) A step-down diagonal line is drawn from the top left to the lower right corner. The inference is that the customers below this line should be shifted above it, i.e., either receive fewer deliveries or buy more milk, or both.

Salesman: *Don Hamill* Route # *9* Supervisor *Buchanan*

DELIVERIES PER MONTH	LESS THAN $5.00	$5.00 to $7.50	$7.50 to $10.00	$10.00 to $12.50	$12.50 to $15.00	$15.00 to $17.50	$17.50 to $20.00	$20.00 or MORE
4 or LESS (27)	23	3	1					
5								
6								
7					141			
8								
9 (194)	59	32	24	12	4	3		
10								
11								
12								
13 (174)	11	33	30	29	22	15	7	22
14								
15		194 OVERSERVICE?						
16 or MORE								

119

Manufacturing and delivering ice to retailers continued to be a commercial undertaking even after refrigerators and freezers became common in American homes. This is a mid-1950s Ford. *Hewitt-Lucas Body Co.*

A mid-1950s International pickup delivering the Detroit News. An extra bar protects the rear window. Note the small poster inside the bracket on the tailgate. The photo was taken in 1963. *American Automobile Manufacturers Association*

A mid-1950s Chevrolet used by REA Express with a body that dropped nearly to the ground to facilitate loading and unloading. *American Truck Historical Society*

A 1956 Ford panel truck, restored and slightly customized, used by a "mailbox/packaging" store. This photo was taken in Scottsdale in 1999.

This truck delivers ginger ale. The front part is from a step-van while the rear is a low, conventional box body. The Hewitt-Lucas Body Co. built the body on a mid-1950s Ford chassis. *Hewitt-Lucas Body Co.*

The Heiser Co. in Seattle built this step-van for a French bread baker. *Geo. Heiser Body Co.*

Looking at the front view we'd guess that this was on a Ford chassis. *Geo. Heiser Body Co.*

A 1957 Chevrolet with a Heiser body used to deliver Meadowsweet dairy products. *Geo. Heiser Body Co.*

This is a Wolfwagon, developed in Dallas in the late 1950s. Original models were little more than semi-trailers with a half cab and powertrain added. Also added was a steering front axle, and one or both of the trailing axles was converted to power. A Wolfwagon could be coupled with another Wolfwagon and operated in tandem by one driver. The model shown here was built by the St. Louis Car Co., under license from Wolf, and was used by Swift and Co. Note the towbar. *American Truck Historical Society*

A circa-1958 International Metro (with different styling than the conventional Metro) that was finished by Marion. *Marion Body Works*

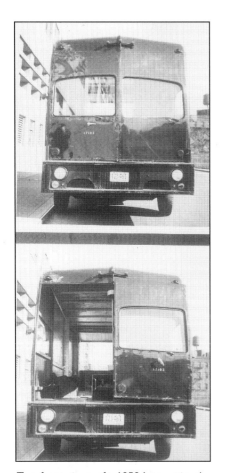

An elevator mounted on the side of a trailer made it easier to handle heavy parcels.

Two front views of a 1958 International, used by UPS. The bottom view shows how half of the front slides to the right to allow access to the cargo compartment. *UPS*

A step-van body on a Dodge chassis, circa 1960. Note the twin rearview mirrors; one is for when the driver is standing, the other for when the driver is sitting.

A 1959 Dodge with a milk body.
National Automotive History Collection, Detroit Public Library

This is White's 1960 "PDQ" model, with the letters standing for "Pickup and Deliver Quickly." *Volvo/White*

Chapter Seven

1961–1970

In the 1950s, Volkswagens gained a toehold in U.S. markets, and one of their products was a truck in a van body. Japanese autos and trucks started appearing on the West Coast. Campers and motor homes were becoming increasingly popular, and some of the truck van chassis that had originally been designed to hold delivery bodies served equally well at holding motor home bodies.

A Boyertown ad for step-van bodies in a 1961 trade journal indicated that they kept a "pool" of popular truck chassis in stock at their Boyertown, Pennsylvania, plant. This meant that their step-van buyers did not have to wait to have the truck chassis shipped from the factory to Boyertown.

More radio frequencies were opened, and some delivery fleets began using radios to dispatch their drivers.

Freihofer's, a large East Coast bakery operation with five plants, retired their last horse from house-to-house delivery in 1962. (In 1972, they would terminate all home deliveries.)

Chevrolet truck literature for 1962 included pictures of two sizes of step-vans with this description: "Step-Vans with bodies 8, 10, and 12 feet long with gross-vehicle-weight (GVW) ratings from 5,600 to 10,000 lbs. Large, roomy interiors and convenient sliding side doors make loading and unloading a breeze. Six forward control chassis are also available for special body installations." That year Chevrolet also offered a

Ed's Flying Service, located at the Alamogordo, New Mexico, airport still uses this 1961 Chevrolet for delivering fuel to aircraft.

full-size step-van with a 7-foot-long body on a 102-inch wheelbase; and a smaller step-van, the "Corvan," built on the Corvair 95-inch wheelbase chassis. Note that these body styles were sold directly by dealers; the buyer did not need to deal also with a truck body builder.

Some years ago Grumman/Olson supplied the writer with a fairly complete set of their 1963 literature. The booklets range from 2 to 24 pages in length. These are the titles: "Aluminum Alloy Bodies by Grumman for 1963 GMC Forward Control Chassis," "A Whale of a Light Body," "Ford Parcel Trucks with Olson Aluminum Bodies," "Olson Aluminum Bodies for Chevrolet Forward Control Chassis," "Olson Kurb Side Aluminum Bodies by Grumman for 1963 Chevrolet Forward Control Models," "Olson Kurb Side Aluminum Bodies by Grumman for 1963 Dodge Forward Control Models," "Golden Economies for Route Deliveries," "Kargo-King Aluminum Alloy Truck Bodies by Grumman" (these were not walk-in bodies), and "Olson Aluminum Alloy Bodies by Grumman Pay for Themselves Thru Savings."

The last booklet also showed a small matching single-axle trailer, with 315 cubic feet for use on "peak load" days. One of the brochures had an accessory price list with dealer's cost and suggested list price (25 percent markup). The accessories consisted of dual rear wheels, various sizes of rear doors, various bulkhead and bulkhead door arrangements, locks with keys for doors, flush directional signals, large heater and defroster, doorless driver's side with roll-down window, various arrangements of diamond-plate flooring, extra dome light on same switch, dual sun visors, right side mirror, dual oblong rearview mirrors, spare tire compartment with rear bumper access, various types of roof vents—some with fans, vents rather than windows in rear doors, extra foam rubber seat, laundry pipe racks, exterior lights to meet Interstate Commerce Commission requirements, grille guard, floor supports, and dual electric windshield wipers.

Wren and Wren reports these developments for the decade:

1961 Chevrolet introduced a "step-van" with 7-foot-stand-up height.

1963 Battronic Truck Corporation and Boyertown Auto Body Works announced a battery-powered delivery truck.

1964 GMC announced a new "Handi-Van," mounted on a 90-inch wheelbase.

1965 Bus and truck production was 1,803,000 units.

1966 Cummins introduced a diesel engine to be used for "stop and go" operations.

1967 Plastics were being used in many trucks to help keep weights and costs down. Fiberglass also had some limited applications.

1968 Ford and Caterpillar Engines announced development of a medium V-8 diesel engine for stop-and-go deliveries.

1969 While diesel engines were becoming more numerous, the V-8 gasoline engine was the most popular one used in trucks.

1970 Federal controls would increase in the areas of emissions and safety. Sales were 1,734,000 trucks and buses.

Wilbur Smith and Associates, transportation planning consultants, surveyed truck travel in the Cincinnati area in 1968, trying to determine patterns of local truck travel. They reported that a typical furnace repair shop used a pickup truck that would leave the shop once or twice each day and make 2–4 calls before returning. A typical dry cleaner operated a panel truck that would leave the dry cleaning shop once or twice a day, but make 14 deliveries before returning to the shop. An auto parts dealer would operate a panel truck that left the shop six times a day and made 1 or 2 stops on each trip before returning. (Note this reflects the nature of the auto parts supply business, a service station may be replacing a customer's muffler and will phone in asking that one be delivered, usually within the hour.) A typical lumber company used a flatbed truck that left the lumber yard three times a day, and made 1–3 drops before returning to the yard. Telephone service trucks were panels, and left their home base once or twice a day, and made 10–15 service stops before returning home. Lastly, milk retailers used vans that left in the morning, made 100 to 125 stops, and returned at night.

In the 1960s, the federal government began upgrading the equipment requirements for ambulances. One requirement dealt with the interior height of the compartment where the stretcher was carried; and the result was that some van-type bodies were designed for ambulance use.

The *Commercial Carrier Journal's* 75th anniversary issue listed these developments during the decade: fiberglass reinforced plywood for bodies and numerous improvements in the components of the drive train. In 1961, Ford introduced its "Econoline" van, a body style that is still in widespread use.

A stand-up body on a 1961 Ford chassis.
Historical Society of Western Pennsylvania

Because of their inside height, step-vans were sometimes converted into mobile homes such as this early-1960s International Metro, which became a "hippiemobile." It was spotted in San Francisco in the late 1970s. The rack on the top suggests that it was probably once a laundry truck.

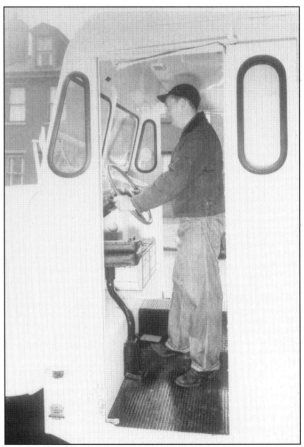

This view inside a step-van shows the driver in a standing position. To the left we see the seat folded forward, and the top down. There is a single pedal on the floor. *Historical Society of Western Pennsylvania*

A 1961 White PDQs used by a Baltimore diaper service. *Volvo/White*

A van with a Marion stand-up body in the early 1960s. *Marion Body Works*

This 1961 White PDQ was used by a Cleveland firm that serviced warehouse and materials-handling equipment. The racks inside hold parts and tools. *Volvo/White*

Wilson & Co., a meat packer, had a cooled body built by Thermo King on a 1962 GMC chassis. *Thermo King Corp.*

Chevrolet made and sold these vans in 1962 and 1963. This one was photographed in Tomales, California, in 1998. The circular pattern on the grille is not original.

An early-1960s Divco, spotted in Sparks, Nevada, in the 1980s.

A 1963 Dodge used by a delivery firm that hauled air freight for several airlines serving the Detroit City Airport. *American Trucking Associations.*

A 1963 GMC with a special body designed for distributing salad dressings. *Geo. Heiser Body Co.*

An insulated dairy body on a 1964 Chevrolet chassis. Note the racks on the top. *Aluminum Truck Bodies of St. Louis*

A 1964 Dodge with a frozen foods body used in Detroit. The cooling unit is above the cab. *American Automobile Manufacturers Association*

A mid-1960s Diamond-T COE used by an electrical supply company in New Jersey.

A step-van body constructed by Heiser of Seattle, nearly ready for placement on a chassis. *Geo. Heiser Body Co.*

A 1965 Studebaker with right-hand drive. Initially it was a mail truck, and then it was used by a janitorial service.

An International step-van, circa 1965–66, used to deliver newspapers in South San Francisco. This photo was taken in the late 1970s during the fuel "crisis." Note the price of gasoline.

This is the rear of a Culligan's truck used to carry cartridges for recharging water softeners in customers' houses. *General Body Company, Chicago*

A late-1960s Dodge armored truck making a pickup at a Michigan bank. *American Trucking Associations*

A 1969 Chevrolet, with a 26-foot van body and 5-foot body extension over the cab, used by a firm that made convertible sofas. *The Truck Gazette*

A late-1960s International flatbed still used by a nursery in Tomales, California.

A 1970 Chevrolet step-van. That year the buyer had the option of aluminum or steel body, and body lengths of 10, 12, or 14 feet. *Chevrolet*

Chapter Eight

1971–1980

This was the decade of several fuel crises that resulted in spot shortages of gasoline and diesel fuels and dramatic increases in their prices. Both private motorists and truck fleet operators had to recalculate their operating costs. Some new autos and light truck models were introduced that were smaller than those sold during the 1960s. Aluminum and plastics became more common in truck bodies, mainly because of their lower weights.

An article in a 1972 dry cleaning industry magazine, based on interviews with fleet managers of three large dry cleaners, described their "wants." One of the three was very interested in adapting his fleet to diesel engines, and he was trying to develop a relationship with Mercedes Benz so that he could test their engine in his trucks. He also spoke of his firm's unsatisfactory experiences with using liquified petroleum gas (LPG) as fuel. The second fleet manager talked about his maintenance operation and said it was qualified to do warranty work for Ford and General Motors. He also described how he had to "beef up" the bodies he bought by adding elements such as additional diamond plating floors, larger heaters, etc. The third debated the merits of leasing vs. buying and said that a truck's high center of gravity made cornering difficult. The three discussed other forms of power, including electric trucks, and trucks propelled by "Wankel" engines (rotary engines that at one time were used in Mazdas).

The railroads' once-cooperatively-owned express trucking pickup and delivery subsidiary, REA Express, went out of business. The firm had once been one of the largest fleet operators in the United States (and, as late as 1962, was operating 13,000 trucks). One of the reasons they fell behind was that UPS was offering better service. UPS was attacked by the U.S. Postmaster General for taking away the post office's parcel post service, but he also conceded that "We [the post office] are damaging five parcels to every one of theirs."

The U.S. Department of Transportation, in an effort to reduce delivery truck usage, conducted studies to determine whether urban freight consolidation points could be located on the fringe of downtown areas. All packages destined for a downtown address would be delivered to this center where they would be consolidated into single shipments for each building. Other studies, aimed more at reducing traffic congestion, looked at making downtown buildings keep their receiving docks open at night so trucks could make deliveries then, when there was less traffic on the streets. Little came of these studies.

A 1971 GMC step-in van with a 12-foot body. It was used as a bread truck and contained bread racks. *The Truck Gazette*

An early-1970s Chevrolet pickup with a fifth wheel for pulling a lightweight twin-axle semi-trailer. Rigs like this were used for local deliveries, rather than on highways. Some camping trailers today ride on pickup fifth wheels. *Hewitt-Lucas Body Co.*

This was also the decade when Fred Smith founded Federal Express, now known as FedEx. It was an air-based small parcel delivery service that initially flew all packages picked up late in the day through a terminal at Memphis. The packages would be sorted there and loaded aboard outgoing planes. The planes would arrive at various cities at sunrise and the packages would be delivered by truck during the morning business hours. When one thinks of FedEx, one thinks of planes, but they also operate an enormous fleet of trucks. They have sophisticated communications and tracking systems and can take much of the credit for the general "speed-up" in the acceptable time standards for business communication.

Throughout the 1970s, in downtown areas, there were bicycle messengers who delivered documents and artwork between various professional offices. In the mid-1990s, when the MTV program *The Real World* was based in San Francisco, one of its characters claimed to be a bike messenger.

A Bell System fleet painting manual, dating from the early 1970s, contained instructions for painting and repainting the dark olive trucks with the Bell System's new four-color scheme. The 68-page manual was printed in full color and two pages were devoted to handcarts, lift trucks, and compressor-trailers. Phone

company trucks had carried printed paper posters, but when the new, four-color scheme was introduced, the manual said:

> Many system companies have been using advertising posters on their vehicles. With the introduction of our new corporate graphics, this policy has been changed.
>
> The new Bell System vehicles are a bright two-tone design with strong identification for the System company. So, it is important that these graphics are not obscured, cluttered or complicated by advertising posters that are a secondary form of communication.
>
> Therefore, no advertising of any kind may appear on Bell System vehicles. This applies to Yellow Pages decals and posters.

In 1972 Grumman/Olson announced the introduction of a refrigerated delivery van. Insulation thickness ranged from 3 to 6 inches depending upon the truck's application. The refrigeration unit was installed at the Grumman/Olson factory. An engine-driven compressor provided in-transit cooling and the unit would be "plugged in" to outlets when at its loading dock. The body could be used on a Chevrolet, Ford,

GMC, or International forward-control chassis.

Different chassis makes could be used. Body builders had to be careful not to offend any chassis builder. Some Grumman/Olson literature of the late 1970s offers an example. The two 12-page brochures have identical covers but the titles differ slightly. One says "Data Book Grumman/Olson Aluminum Truck Bodies on Ford Chassis" while the other says "Data Book Grumman/Olson Aluminum Truck Bodies on Chevrolet Chassis." The interior pages look almost the same. The line drawings apparently cover bodies on either chassis. The tables of measurements differ slightly, because the two makes of chassis have slightly different wheelbases. The photos used differ, although to the untrained eye it's difficult to see a difference in most bodies. Some chassis makes are identifiable; they are the ones where a van body's commercial chassis was used and is identifiable back to the cowl. Pictures of body features were about the same and included reinforced, rounded top corners; side entrance steps with tread plates; aluminum rear bumpers; reinforced rear doors; and aluminum strap hinges with grease fittings. Pictured options were similar, although not identical, and included various shelving, liner, and bulkhead arrangements; grille guard; full range of rear doors (including double doors, four-piece doors, and roll-up door, and choice of windows); bread racks; jump seat; air conditioning; pipe racks (for dry cleaning); and wire mesh bulkhead (with or without a lock). It was also possible to order a body with no door on the left, to keep the driver from walking into traffic. A third piece of literature covered Grumman/Olson bodies on GMC chassis and was fairly similar to the literature describing their bodies on Chevrolets.

The brochures offered different models, although it's hard to say how different. Both offered a "Kurbette" body, which kept the chassis builder's van body back to the cowl. The Ford-oriented brochure devoted three pages to Kabmasters, with the main difference being body widths, 78, 86, and 93 inches. In the Chevrolet-oriented booklet, these were called Kurbmasters and had the same three widths. The Ford-oriented brochure devoted one page to the Kurbmaster King, which could be built on a chassis with a 166-, 184-, or 202-inch wheelbase (while the Kabmasters were on wheelbases of either 138 or 158 inches).

Milestones for the decade reported by Wren and Wren include:

1971 For the first time, annual production of trucks and buses exceeded 2 million units.

1973 The first "energy crisis" took place. Truck sales now exceeded 3 million units, although this was due in part to the increased use of pickup trucks and vans for personal passenger transportation. Clark Equipment introduced a mini-trailer to be used with a fifth-wheel-equipped pickup.

1974 The postal service gave AM General a contract for 350 1/4-ton electric mail delivery trucks.

1975 Both Dodge and Ford introduced new parcel vans.

1976 Congress made a large appropriation for electric vehicle research.

1977 Volvo introduced some mid-size city delivery trucks into the U.S. market.

1978 Truck builders were under great pressure to produce trucks that consumed less fuel, produced fewer emissions, and met stricter safety standards.

1979 Several manufacturers offered fuel-saving diesel engines for their light trucks.

1980 The interstate trucking industry was deregulated, which would result in many changes in its economic structure.

Throughout the century, trucks making deliveries became larger. One reason was the growth of large "mass merchandisers" who controlled many stores. In addition, most new retail stores were large in terms of floor space, so they also could handle larger sizes of shipments.

An early-1970s Ford step-van used by a roofing contractor and spotted in 1998 parked along a Wisconsin highway with a "for sale" sign.

A 1973 Ford walk-in van, with a 10-foot body, on a used truck lot. *The Truck Gazette*

A 1973 Ford C-series with an ice-cream body, used by a St. Louis firm. *Aluminum Truck Bodies, St. Louis*

Orowheat used this semi-trailer to carry racks of bread for its chain-store customers. There is a winch inside the trailer that raises and lowers the wheeled rack from the trailer. *Utility Trailer Manufacturing Co.*

Nearly all the photos in this book deal with trucks built and used within the United States. Auto and truck makers were aware of worldwide markets, however, and expanded into them as best they could. Initially, much of the world could not afford U.S.-built vehicles. General Motors' subsidiary in Malaysia assembled this delivery truck there in the early 1970s, and it was used by a firm that sold cord for sewing tops of bags. The body was made in Malaysia in a deliberate low-tech manner. The pattern was laid out on a thin sheet of steel, cut out using little more than tin-snips, and then creased into position. This is not unlike some of the figures one once made from characters printed on the sides of cereal boxes. *GM*

A 1974 Chevrolet with a refrigerated van body. *The Truck Gazette*

This is a 1974 Ford Econovan with a 12-foot refrigerated body. *The Truck Gazette*

A 1970s Ford step-van used by a cheesesteaks distributor in San Jose.

This 1976 Chevrolet had a refrigerated body and was used for distributing meat and cheese. *The Truck Gazette*

A circa-1976 Chevrolet van chassis with a furniture body, operating in Auburn, California.

The bulge at the front of the body is a wind deflector (despite what the sign says about "pregnant"). The chassis is a mid-1970s International, and the truck was used to distribute nursery furniture in Southern California. *Trucking Equipment Supply Co., San Francisco*

A Grumman step-van on a Chevrolet chassis parked adjacent to a Nevada highway and carrying advertisements for filling stations and a convenience store.

A late-1970s Dodge van chassis with a Mark-built body installed on the rear. *Mark Body*

A hydraulic scissors-lift body used for an airline catering truck, mounted on a late-1970s Ford chassis. The body was built by Tesco. *Truck and Equipment Service, Fort Lauderdale*

An Olson Kurbmaster from the late 1970s, spotted at a beer fest in San Jose, California. It carried materials for a booth and a back-up supply of Coors.

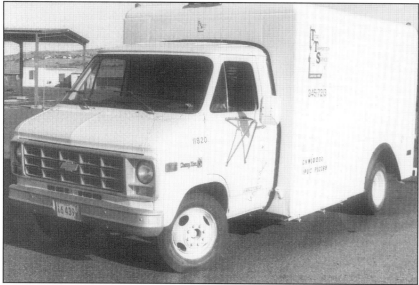

A 1979 Chevrolet van chassis with a cargo box, used by a firm called Total Transportation Systems. *The Truck Gazette*

A tire delivery, installation, and service body built on a 1979 Ford pickup. It has a powered tailgate. *Iowa Mold Tooling*

A 1979 GMC step-van of a model that was sold directly by GMC dealers. *The Truck Gazette*

This was the 1980 Grumman/Olson Kurbmaster which, according to the company's press release, could be built on either a Chevrolet or GMC chassis in body widths of 78 inches, 86 inches, and 93 inches, and on wheelbases from 125 inches to 157 inches. The press release also stressed that the aluminum bodies were lighter in weight and more fuel efficient, a matter of great concern at that time. *Grumman/Olson*

Two Grumman/Olson step-vans, circa 1980. *The Truck Gazette*

Chapter Nine

1981 to the Present

In 1982, the transportation committee of the American Bakers Association decided that they were unhappy with the current bakery delivery trucks. They claimed that the typical bakery route truck was a "motor home clone," and that the motor home builders were interested in power and comfort, rather than a million-mile life cycle.

Many of the trucks bought during this period are still on the road. The van style of delivery truck, using a body supplied by the chassis builder, seems to be popular. Most news regarding UPS and FedEx involves their aircraft fleets and their expansion into overseas markets, where they must coordinate and operate truck fleets worldwide. The ubiquitous brown UPS truck can be spotted in major cities almost anywhere in the world.

In 1998 FedEx operated a fleet of about 40,000 trucks worldwide while UPS operated nearly 160,000. UPS, FedEx, and DHL all expanded their operations overseas. During much of the 1990s, they ran national

television commercials advertising these expanded services. A UPS strike in 1997 demonstrated how dependent some of their customers were.

Niche players survived. All the other parcel carriers, the U.S. Postal Service, UPS, and FedEx are set for overnight service. An article in a 1998 issue of *Transport Topics* described local trucking services in Traverse City, Michigan, that made same-day deliveries. "These days, because of faxes, delivery services get few calls for document delivery, but there is still good trade in carrying print jobs for printers, business records headed to and from storage, mail pickups, lunch orders for day care centers, dentures for dental labs, and, yes, even livestock if it is caged and the cage fits in the vans." A lady in the area has service for elderly clients. "She does their grocery shopping, picks up prescriptions, takes pets to the vet, picks up dry-cleaning, does their banking and much more."

One body-building firm that has grown throughout this period is Utilimaster of Wakarusa, Indiana, which was founded in 1973 as a spin-off from the recreational vehicle industry (which was in the doldrums because of the fuel crisis). In 1995 the firm received a three-year contract to be the sole supplier of FedEx vehicles, and in the same year, worked with a GMC dealer to provide 1,900 walk-in vans for the U.S. Postal Service. In 1998, the firm became a subcontractor to Ford Motor Company to build 10,500 carrier route vehicles for the Postal Service. A company release described its marketing structure: "Utilimaster markets its products directly to approximately 150 National and Fleet Accounts (National Accounts

A hydraulic lift gate on a 1981 Chevrolet pickup. Note that two of the kitchen appliances are kept strapped to a dolly when loaded, carried, and unloaded. *Peabody-Galion*

Purolator Courier Corp. used this 1981 Ford van for its deliveries. On the right-hand rear door below the name is a bracket that holds a hazardous materials warning diamond. *3M*

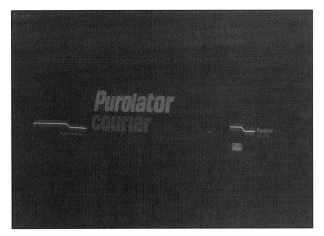

This is a night photo showing the reflectorized sign and license plate. *3M*

typically have 1,000+ vehicle fleets and Fleet Accounts typically have 100+ vehicle fleets), and through independent dealers who resell the Company's vehicles to commercial end users (Commercial Accounts). The Company's in-house sales force is divided into four sales segments (Parcel, Baking/Snack, Cleaning/Industrial, and Commercial)." They state that their major competitors for walk-in vans include Grumman/Olson and Union City Body Co.

During this entire decade there was renewed interest in delivery trucks that were powered by batteries or various alternative fuels. This interest was spurred by a California requirement that auto manufacturers begin selling some of these vehicles in the next century. Delivery trucks are often ideal users of electric batteries since their routes are known in advance and during the nights they are not in use and hence can be recharged. A December 23, 1997, release reported on the World Wide Web said, in part: "Despite unseasonably cold and inclement weather, Solectria Corporation's newest electric vehicle—the Solectria CitiVan, a walk-in zero-emission delivery truck—was warmly received last week during its public debut at the . . . international electric vehicle symposium in Orlando, Florida. . . . The Solectria CitiVan incorporates a chassis built by General Motors, a body manufactured by the Union City Body Company, and electric vehicle . . . components designed and produced by Solectria, including a complete electric drive system and an on-board battery charger. General Motors has agreed to provide 'gliders'

(engine-less chassis) to Solectria, and to honor service and warranty commitments on the chassis of the Solectria CitiVan. The Solectria CitiVan is designed for delivery service in urban settings where air quality concerns are paramount. It is ideal for short route, stop-and-go travel associated with a variety of typical delivery applications."

The markets for delivery services, and vehicles, are expected to remain strong. One reason is that more people are working at home and expect to have documents and other materials delivered to their door. Also, in many households, both adults must now work, giving them less time to run errands themselves; they must rely on others.

UPS began using body designs that masked the name and identifying symbols of the chassis builder. Here's a UPS truck, outfitted by Mark Body of Mt. Clemens, Michigan, in the early 1980s. *Mark Body*

A mid-1980s Dodge pickup with a large body extending over the cab. *Brown Cargo Van, Inc.*

A dry cleaner in Yuma, Arizona, uses this mid-1980s Chevrolet Astro van.

Three circa-1986 Dodges used by a floral shop in Palm Desert, California.

A 1987–88 Navistar International tank truck used in Kewaunee, Wisconsin. On both the front and sides are red hazardous materials placards with the number "1203," meaning gasoline. If the truck were to be in an accident, firefighters arriving on the scene would note the number "1203" and would consult manuals dealing with how to contain and manage the spill.

Airborne Express used this late-1980s Ford for package pickup and delivery. *Airborne Freight Corporation*

A restored UPS 1929 Ford A used in a publicity shot at the time UPS added some Boeing all-cargo planes to its fleet. UPS has a number of restored trucks, kept at various sites throughout the United States. *UPS*

This circa-1989 Navistar International was used by a co-op in Kewaunee, Wisconsin. It has several fuel tanks and their capacities are painted across the top of the tank.

A circa-1990 GMC van chassis with a large cargo box distributing printed materials in Sedona, Arizona.

A small replica of an old truck spotted near San Diego in the early 1990s.

An early-1990s Ford van used by FedEx.

Supreme Corp. of Goshen, Indiana, built the furniture body for this circa-1992 Ford 350, spotted in Yuma, Arizona.

Joe Doty owns this 1992 Mitsubishi and makes deliveries for Dominos in the Rancho Mirage, California, area. Most pizza deliveries are made in private autos supplied by young workers. In recent years "guaranteed-time deliveries" for pizzas were subject to criticism since they were not completely compatible with safe driving practices.

Brown Cargo Van in Lawrence, Kansas, built this van for a medical and welding supplies distributor on an early-1990s Navistar chassis. Barely visible in the lower center of the body are two brackets for holding hazardous materials placards. *Brown Cargo Van, Inc.*

A dairy equipment distributor in Lawrence, Kansas, used this Brown body on a 1993–94 Navistar International chassis. The door at the front of the cargo box is low. *Brown Cargo Van, Inc.*

A medium-size Ford used by Airborne Express for trips between airports and city terminals. In 1998, Airborne operated 14,300 trucks, all radio-dispatched. *Airborne Freight Corporation*

A 1994 Ford used by DHL Worldwide Express, an international parcel carrier. *DHL*

A Brown-built insulated body with a Carrier refrigeration unit on a 1995 Kenworth chassis. *Brown Cargo Van, Inc.*

A mid-1990s Mitsubishi Fuso used by a Santa Rosa, California, home appliance store.

This 1996 Dodge pickup has an aluminum utility body. The parts cabinets would be used by craftsmen performing home repairs or installations. *Alum-Line, Inc.*

A late-1990s Ford van chassis with a Utilimaster body with an "aerocap" feature that provides aerodynamic styling above the cab. *Utilimaster*

A vending body with roll-up side doors built by Utilimaster. *Utilimaster*

A circa-1997 Toyota Tacoma pickup with a body shell used by a donut shop in Auburn, California.

Bibliography

American Automobile Manufacturers Association. *Motor Vehicle Facts & Figures,* 1998 (Detroit: the association, 1998).

Autac literature, circa 1978.

Baldwin, Nick. *Old Delivery Vans* (Aylesbury, Bucks, United Kingdom: Shire Publications, 1987).

Bartlett, John T. "Advertising Aspects of Truck Painting," *The Automobile Trimmer and Painter,* October 1925, pages 53–54.

———. "The Possibilities In Colors for Truck Advertising," *The Automobile Trimmer and Painter,* March 1925, pages 67–68.

Bell System Vehicle Graphics Manual (New York: A T & T, 1975).

Benson, H. L. "The Art of Vehicle Painting," *The Automobile Trimmer and Painter,* March 1926, pages 42–43.

Burness, Tad. *American Truck & Bus Spotter's Guide 1920–1985* (Osceola, Wis.: MBI Publishing Company, 1985).

———. *Pickup and Van Spotter's Guide 1945–1982* (Osceola, Wis.: Motorbooks International, 1982).

Caffrey, Charlotte. "The Perfect Truck," *Linen Supply News,* March 1972, pages 21–28, 32–36.

Clark of Oshkosh body literature, circa 1930.

Cottrell, James W. "The Horse Myth Gets the Stable," *The Commercial Car Journal,* September 1929, pages 13–16, 60.

Crismon, Fred W. *International Trucks* (Osceola, Wis.: MBI Publishing Company, 1995).

Daniel Jr., J. M. *Hackney: the history of a company* (Wilson, N.C.: the Hackney company, 1979).

"Designing the Route Truck of the Future," *The Private Carrier,* January 1988, pages 33–34.

"Door-to-Door Units Promote the Trend to Direct Selling," *The Commercial Car Journal,* April 1933, pages 18–20.

Duggan, Edward P. "The Education of American carriage makers, 1880–1916," *The Journal of Transport History,* March 1990, pages 1–11.

Dunbar, W. T. "DeLuxe Delivery Body with Town Car Front," *Motor Body, Paint and Trim,* July 1932, pages 7–8, 22.

———. "Salt-and-Ice Ice-Cream Body with Cork Insulation," *Motor Body, Paint and Trim,* January 1932, pages 9–11.

Ebert, Robert R., and John S. Rienzo Jr. *Divco—A History of the Truck and Company* (Yellow Springs, Ohio: Antique Power, 1997).

Echlin, Bill. "Can't Get It the Same Day? Let the Local Guys Do It," *Transport Topics,* March 2, 1998, page 28.

"Exhibitors Film Delivery plays leading role—from package express to hauling films," *The Kansas Transporter,* May 1976, pages 8–11.

Facts and Figures of the Automobile Industry (Detroit: National Automobile Chamber of Commerce, 1932).

"Freihofer's: family baking tradition since 1886," *Milling & Baking News,* August 23, 1977, no page numbers.

"The Golden Years of Highway Transportation," *The Commercial Car Journal,* 50th Anniversary Special edition, 1961.

Grumman/Olson literature, various years.

Hercules body literature, 1932.

Herman Body Company literature, circa 1950.

Hackney Bros. literature, various years.

Hewitt-Lucas Body Company literature, various years.

The History of Nabisco Brands, Inc. (East Hanover, N. J.: the company, 1981).

International Metro literature, circa 1955.

Johnson, Ben. "The Story of Field's Delivery Service," *The Field Glass,* May 26, 1941, pages 4–5.

Laycock, George. *The Kroger Story* (Cincinnati: the company, 1983).

Mark Body literature, circa 1980.

Martin-Parry body literature, 1926–1930.

McMillan, A. G. *Model A/AA Ford Truck Owner* (Arcadia, Calif.: Post-Era Books, 1975).

"Milestones in Trucking," *The Commercial Carrier Journal,* March 1986.

Milligan Truck Body Co. literature, circa 1950.

"Motor Truck Dealers Make Good Profits by Selling Standardized Truck Bodies with Chassis," *The Commercial Car Journal,* June 15, 1919, pages 31–50.

Motor Truck Facts (Detroit: Automobile Manufacturers Association, 1949).

Motor Trucks in the Metropolis (New Haven: Wilbur Smith and Associates, 1969).

Mroz, Albert. *The Illustrated Encyclopedia of American Trucks and Commercial Vehicles* (Iola, Wis.: Krause, 1996).

"Multi-Stop Units Dub Dobbin A Dud," *The Commercial Car Journal,* April 1932, pages 18–21.

"Olson Introduces Refrigerated Delivery Truck," *Refrigerated Transporter,* November 1972, no page numbers.

"Package from Field's" *The Field Glass,* September 4, 1951, pages 4–6.

Perry, Harry W. "The Commercial Motor Truck vs. the Horse; a comparison of efficiencies and costs," *Scientific American,* January 14, 1911, pages 36–37, 50.

Rawson, Bart. "Inside UPS," *The Commercial Car Journal,* March 1973, no page numbers.

Rittenhouse, Jack D. *American Horse-Drawn Vehicles* (New York: Bonanza, 1948).

Rock Hill Body Co. literature, various dates.

Rose, Floyd A. "How the Body Shop Can Profit with Decalcomania Transfers," *The Automobile Trimmer and Painter,* February 1935, pages 20–23.

Sandberg, Lars J. *Truck Selling: simultaneous selling and delivery in wholesale food distribution,* Harvard University Graduate School of Business Administration Business Research Study No. 7, circa 1935.

Shondell, W. Joseph. "History of Fleet Graphics," *The Private Carrier,* June 1985, pages 34, 37.

Siuru, Bill, and Brian Siuru. "Sedan Deliveries—more than a car, less than a truck," *Old Cars News & Marketplace,* Dec. 6, 1990, page 5.

Solectria Corporation press release, December 23, 1997.

Special Bodies on the Speed Wagon Chassis (Lansing, Reo Motor Car Company, 1922).

Staley, Richard A. "Fleet Marking Advantages, Your trucks are you . . . Why not say so?" *The Private Carrier,* June 1984, pages 34–36.

Stewart Truck Bodies, Inc. literature, circa 1941.

Tesco Hi-Lift Truck & Equipment Service Co. literature, circa 1980.

Timpte, Inc. literature, various years.

United Automotive Body Co. literature, circa 1922.

Utilimaster literature, circa 1998.

Weaver, John D. *Carnation, the first 75 years* (Los Angeles: the company, 1974).

West, Bill. "W. Everett Miller, Designer and Engineer," *Wheels of Time,* March/April 1984, pages 12–13.

"Where Did the Wolfwagons Go?" *American Truck Historical Society Newsletter,* April 1977, page 2.

"White PDQ (Pickup and Deliver Quickly)," *Power Wagon,* April 1960, no page numbers.

Wood, Donald F. "A Brief History of Productmobiles," *Special-Interest Autos,* number 147, 1995, pages 46–51.

———. *Beverage Trucks 1910–1975 Photo Archive* (Osceola, Wis.: Iconografix, 1996).

———. "Boulevard Deliveries," *Wheels of Time,* Vol. 5, No. 2, 1984, pages 26–27.

———. "Carting Coal," *Special-Interest Autos,* number 45, 1978, pages 40–45.

———. *Commercial Trucks* (Osceola, Wis.: MBI Publishing Companyl, 1993).

———. "Ice Trucks We've Known and Loved," *Special-Interest Autos,* number 46, 1978, pages 50–54.

———. "Just One Quart Today," *Special-Interest Autos,* number 31, 1975, pages 39–43.

———. "Stores on Wheels," *Special-Interest Autos,* number 43, 1978, pages 26–29, 64.

——. "The Business Cycle," *American Motorcyclist,* Vol. 40, No. 9, 1986, pages 23–27.

———. "The Driver/Salesman and His Changing Role," *Papers, Transportation Research Forum,* 1973 (Oxford, Indiana: Richard B. Cross, 1973), pages 631–637.

Wren, James A., and Genevieve J. Wren. *Motor Trucks of America* (Ann Arbor, Mich.: University of Michigan Press, 1979).